D1740200

Faces at the Window

Maurice Wiggin

Nelson

Thomas Nelson and Sons Ltd
36 Park Street London WIY 4DE
PO Box 18123 Nairobi Kenya

Thomas Nelson (Australia) Ltd
597 Little Collins Street Melbourne 3000

Thomas Nelson and Sons (Canada) Ltd
81 Curlew Drive Don Mills Ontario

Thomas Nelson (Nigeria) Ltd
PO Box 336 Apapa Lagos

Thomas Nelson and Sons (South Africa) (Proprietary) Ltd
51 Commissioner Street Johannesburg

© Maurice Wiggin 1972

First published 1972

0 17 142013 6

Printed in Great Britain by
Northumberland Press Ltd Gateshead

Preface

THIS is not by any means a complete gallery of portraits: there are several conspicuous empty spaces, you can see the faded patches where the pictures hung. Why are these people missing?

Some because I have already written about them, to such an extent that I could not bear to repeat myself. I have written elsewhere about my parents, my wife, my boyhood friend Hardy; about Tom and Fannie Westwood, sweetest and saintliest couple I ever knew; about Joe Harper, Harry Walford, the remarkable Smith family of Bloxwich, 'Uncle' Joe Simpson Hall, Harvey Ellingham, Ivan Roe, Tim Solly, Lily Butler, and a number of others who have meant a lot in my life and whom I remember still with nothing but affection. They belong here, but must be sought elsewhere.

Then there are those, both eminent and obscure, about whom one's feelings have changed.... I do not wish to take a stealthy revenge on affection for having failed me. Some friendships which seem unshakeable prove impermanent. Not that this is wholly a book of friendships, but neither is it a book of cherished enmities.

Missing are a number of public faces, which, when it came down to it, I found myself unable to sketch in with the charity

I would hope for myself. So in the end I omitted those bitter drafts, etched in acid. I cannot help it if my respect and admiration and affection for the people whom I have known is sometimes in inverse proportion to their eminence and power and wealth. But I did not wish for the ephemeral notoriety of bitchy iconoclasm. Nor for the trivial renown of name-dropping, which I might do as well as most.

It isn't even, strictly speaking, a gallery of portraits, though it was meant to be. Sketches, shall we say? I cannot always discern with wished-for clarity the lineaments of these revenants who have passed, and pass again, the window at which the onlooker sits, in a trance of recollection. But I can hear their voices, I recognise those footfalls, and if some are shadowy, they are still faces I seem to know. My wish is that they should recognise themselves.

I

Up the Street

THE Street was where the life was. Such as it was. It was a wide straight street and a good half mile long, with the Church at one end, opposite the Co-op, and the Park at the other end, laid out and fenced in on both sides of the road. It terminated at the Terminus or as everybody, including tram conductors, said, the Bell. Meaning a boozer called 'The Bell'. The Park (on both sides, do you mind?) took up a lot of valuable building land and gave an air of spaciousness to the Street. Yes, it was a very fine Park and a credit to one and all. The smaller piece of Park on the East side was full of flower beds and not a lot of fun, but the larger part on the West side was mainly grass with clumps of shrubs and trees and a bandstand, and some fun was had there, take my word for it, at various hours of night and day.

Knock off the Park, and the Street as a street, meaning a shopping street, was a lot less than half a mile long, say a quarter. Though there *were* shops along Park Side, the sidelong extension of the Street which veered off behind the flower Park and led to Lichfield Road at an angle. My mother was born on Park Side and so was my wife's mother. There was a shop along there where they sold locusts. Nowadays I can't get anyone to believe it or even show much interest, but we used to eat locusts when we were kids during the Great War. They were a sort of black, dried bean, quite like a broad bean that has been left out far too long. You chewed away for ages at the tough, fibrous locust bean, and the sweetness within was indescribable. You got a huge handful for a ha'penny. A halfpenny. Half an old penny. Say a third of one of today's half-pennies. Even though the old girl who kept this shop, which sold a few vegetables and a bit of fruit to the less well-heeled, was in our eyes a ferocious crone, you still got a good handful for a ha'penny, dug out of a hessian sack which stood by the open door. It was a comedown, it was definitely *infra dig.*, to be seen eating locusts, or as we said, locusses; can't think why it was, but it was; you knew such things.

Just the other day I came across Mr Thomas Joy's delicious autobiography, *Mostly Joy*, and was delighted to discover that he too bought locusts when a child, in Oxford. He tells us that the locust is the Carob bean from the Algorraba tree, grows in Portugal and Majorca and Southern France, and 'is called the locust because it is supposed to have been the food of John the Baptist in the wilderness (Matt. 3:4). It is also called St John's bread'. Thank you, Thomas, you darling man, and may your memoirs never be out of print or out of stock.

No, Park Side was definitely a sideline: the Street began in all its glory at Percy Lawrence's on the corner of Wolverhampton Road, opposite the bus station. Thereafter on both sides it was all go and commerce and life. Well, I say *life* ... actually it was strictly shops, chapels, and a few pubs. Not a billiard room; not a beauty parlour; not a restaurant nor a café. There *had* been a café, of sorts, still remembered as the Coffee Shop, even after it became a sweet shop, just by the flicks. The Misses Wilkes tried again, opening the Parkside Café by the Wesleyan Chapel, but again it didn't catch on, though long after it had ceased to be a café, and become a cake shop, they kept the name. It gave a bit of tone, a wistful touch of class. I think we always felt we ought to have a café on the Street, but there just weren't enough of us with the leisure, or the nerve, to while away the time brazenly drinking tea or coffee in public. Café society never got going in Bloxwich, while I lived there. I don't think it was wholly a question of economics, even in the economic climate of the time. It was more a question of propriety. If you weren't busy

you were sinful. Wasting time was frowned on. A lot of it was being wasted by the unemployed, of course, but somehow that only
made it worse. There were plenty of coffee shops down in Walsall
for those who wanted to idle their time away frivolously. It was
different in that glittering city, where anything went. In Bloxwich
the Lord was watching with a sharp eye for idlers. I think we
felt, obscurely, that if we idled when we might have been working
He'd see to it pretty sharp that we joined the permanent involuntary idlers, the unemployed.

But if we were short of establishments designed for frivolous
idling, we were far from short of shops and chapels, and in those
myriad shops and chapels the social life of the industrial village-
town flowed strongly. I don't know how the population supported
so many, of both sorts. But we were staunch individualists, and
would rather have a lot of little shops and chapels than a few big
ones. I dare say it's different now.

My own favourite shop was Percy Lawrence's, the cycle shop
which was so much more. Percy or Perce was in on bicycles at
an early date in the bicycling era, and he went on from bikes to
motorcycles and cars; for a long time he had a monopoly. Percy
or Perce was a very handsome man, with gingery hair; a sharpish
sort of handsomeness, long of chin, with a slightly sergeant-
majorish moustache. I never saw him without a cap, a sporting
sort of cap. He was a rather dashing sort of man, was Perce,
quite tweedy. One of his characteristics was a high light voice,
strange among so many gruff bass voices. He was quite a
distinctive character.

Early on he secured a pioneering monopoly with a fleet of
hire cars, for funerals and weddings. Unless I'm much mistaken
my parents were carried to and from their wedding, and to their
funerals, in Lawrence vehicles. I could be wrong about the
funerals, though I fancy I travelled in a Lawrence Rolls-Royce
on those occasions. Earlier on it was Minervas and Daimlers,
which were, you will remember, the favourites of Royalty before
Rolls-Royce ever got a nose in. Percy was a sleeve-valve
enthusiast and apart from the rare Minervas he had Daimlers
just like King George's and Queen Mary's Daimlers, and probably he had Daimlers just like King Edward's and Queen
Alexandra's Daimlers, though that was a little before mai taime.

Percy had a son named Harold who married Flo Keay who

used to astonish the village by driving these huge Daimlers, as big as lorries, during the Great War. Flo was a beautiful girl, sensational, and her courage in taking on a man's job like that was the talk of the town. Later she and Harold left and took over the hire car business, and I believe they still run it, and if so good luck to them and many blessings.

Then there was Arthur, who broke with the family tradition by going to the grammar school and on to university and into the professions, though I can't recall which profession. Next came Frank, who toiled in the family business and still runs it, though on a different site: my sister Janet and her husband Bill Howes are still customers of Frank Lawrence, which makes a fairly long unbroken family tradition, nearer seventy than sixty years. I remember Frank riding his New Imperial in local trials and I fear I gave him some trouble with my motorbikes when the time came. Lastly, on my age level more or less, came Girly, the only Lawrence daughter, another attractive lass. I think it's probably fair to say that as a village we bred more pretty girls than handsome men, or perhaps it's just that to my susceptible eyes most girls were more attractive than most chaps.

I spent a great deal of my time at and around Lawrence's, poking about among the vast conglomeration of old cars and stuff which Percy accumulated in his huge sheds. Well, they seemed huge, perhaps they weren't really. But they must have covered a lot of ground; his premises went right through back to Samuel Street—'unadopted', a quagmire in wet weather—and it was not unknown for boys and girls to sneak in, which was easy, and have a cuddle in the back seat of a derelict Daimler or super-annuated Standard. There weren't so many places to go for a cuddle. Of course it's all swept away now.

The Wiggins as a clan were long-time customers of Percy Lawrence: what should we have done without each other? My wife's parents might have been, too, but took against him when, having sold them two new bicycles, one each, he refused to give them a bell between them. It's little things like that that get remembered, never mind literature.

Moving up the Street from Percy's, the first of several butchers was Bilson's, later Bilson & Boot. Mrs Bilson wore dark blue glasses in gold-wire rims, and her hair was scraped tightly back and screwed up in a bun. It gave the old dear a formidable appearance, especially when she was brandishing a butcher's knife, which she could do pretty dexterously. My mother was a regular customer at Bilson's in so far as she could be said to be a regular customer *anywhere*: many and many a time we've eaten a dinner bought from three separate butchers. Ma just liked getting around, I guess, spreading her patronage thin and making the most of the social occasion.

I'm thinking now of Mr Browell the butcher, whose shop was a gleaming new edifice on the site of Tomkinson's old radio and electrical shop. There was a big re-building do and they put up a new Post Office, and Mr Browell's new shop, while Mr Tomkinson crossed the street and went into the stationery and newspaper business. The original stationer was Wheeler's, near Holder's the draper's, run by a real lady, Mrs Wheeler, whom I associate with the blue rinse, though I'm pretty sure the blue rinse hadn't been invented then or at any rate hadn't reached Bloxwich.

The more I think of the old place the more clear it becomes that there was a powerful element of matriarchy, if not downright feminism. Women's Lib may not have been heard of but there were some formidably autocratic wives and some formidably effective female business bosses. Mrs Wheeler was one: she had the knack of making me feel uncouth, which wasn't all that difficult, really. Mrs Bilson was another. The Misses Holmes and Hulme put their genteel signboard up over yet another draper's; ladies ran Brown's and Turner's haberdasheries, which, curiously enough, were next door to one another. Mrs Alden ran the paper, sweets and ciggy shop – yet another, there were dozens. *BDV – A smoke for MEN, not Boys!* it said in enamel on a tin sheet screwed to the wall. Mrs Adams ran the tripe shop next door to the bank. Mrs Cooper had a great say in the running of Cooper's, yet another butcher's. My wife's aunt Ma Leese ran and owned Leese's the pork butcher's famed for tripe, trotters, and black ('pig's') pudding. Mrs Keay ran Jack Keay's little shop next door to our house on the corner of Broad Lane. Madame Morris the celebrated concert artiste, when she retired from public performance, opened yet another draper's next to Taylor's cake shop and almost opposite Tanky Reynold's fish shop. I'm sure I've forgotten a number: it was a place where men were conspicuously men, and wanted you to know it, but women were by no means kept in the background. I know my ma ran us, and I've a feeling that women pretty well ran Bloxwich, or at least were full and equal citizens with their fingers on the till, never mind the ballot box.

Talking of the ballot box, I wonder what became of Rhoda Cartwright? A walk up the Street without seeing Rhoda was a walk wasted, or so I thought at one phase in the old emotional history. Rhoda's dad was the first Labour councillor I ever heard of. Suddenly the place was alive with yellow, red and black posters and leaflets that said—

VOTE FOR DAN
THE PEOPLE'S MAN

I thought that was absolutely spot-on; thought it made the old reactionary propaganda look effete and stuffy. We were still Liberals, hadn't gone bolshie yet (later my father followed Dan on to Walsall Borough Council as a Labour councillor, causing scandal among the faithful) but we sneakingly sympathised with this first working-man politician and were delighted if shocked when he actually got in, breaking the 'reactionary' ring. Not everyone was delighted. Copies of Dan's electioneering posters, neatly torn into squares, the size of toilet paper, were found in the lavatories of Elmore Green Girls' School – the work of unscrupulous political opponents, no doubt. I know of this as a fact – I don't mean I know who did it, but I know it was done – because my wife and Rhoda were in the same class. Rhoda laughed it off, and I've no doubt Dan did, too. He had to take a lot of razzing.

Strange it may seem, at this moment in history, but our first radical working-class politician went about dressed in a black jacket, striped trousers and a bowler hat. Not very revolutionary. Actually he was a keen and indefatigable councillor who stuck up for his constituents, and they knew he did, even if he never became Mayor when it was his due. He wasn't a rabble-rouser with the style of one of those radicals from the Pleck or Palfrey, whose famous slogan, shouted at mass meetings, was 'Yo' stick to me, and I'll stick to yo', like snot sticks to a cinder'.

I mustn't forget Reg Henderson the jeweller, in whose shop I spent scores if not hundreds of hours, just leaning on the counter watching the world go by, ever my favourite occupation. It was he who provided me with the actual peg, the tenuous and unlikely introduction, which launched me into journalism. Goodness, he was long-suffering; I do owe him a debt.

I mustn't forget Hodson's either, and I'm not likely to. Tommy Hodson ran this tailoring and outfitting shop, with his brother Charlie. Charles was slender, dark and shy, Tom was sturdy, lighter in colouring; they were both very good-looking in different ways entirely. I had my very first suit from Hodson's – a grey flannel two-piece which so ravished me that I wore it all the way home and burst into tears when required to take it off ('for Sunday best') and revert to the blue woollen jersey and nondescript tough-wearing shorts of everyday. Tom also supplied some very peculiar garments – not that it was his fault – which mother thought suitable, from time to time, for a growing young bourgeois. Mother's irrepressible urge for buying retail in small quantities and at different times landed me with several outfits, during my schooldays, which caused a certain amount of suffering; such as the brown serge trousers worn with a brown serge jacket of a slightly but perceptibly different shade. Do you wonder I never grew into a dandy? At one stage, when I was about fifteen, and just getting really self-conscious and girl-mad, mother went berserk and bought me a black jacket and striped sponge-bag trousers, as worn by solicitors. It took some living down, especially when worn to school with a grey worsted home-knitted jersey, yellow-black-and-green school tie and cap, and brown boots.

I went berserk myself one day a few years later, while I was an undergrad at Oxford. The family had left me at home while they went to Rhyl for the annual hol – I don't remember if it was meant as a punishment for some misdemeanour, or a reward – and I spotted in Hodson's, while killing time talking to Tom and Charles instead of swotting, a two-piece tweed plus-four suit, marked down to £2 in the summer sale. They must have had it on their hands for years. I simply couldn't resist it and said, 'Put it on the account'. There was hell to pay when they all got back and found me parading the Street in plus-fours. I had to wear them until they were in rags, but that wasn't long. At £2?

Tommy was a motor enthusiast and his cars, parked all day right there in the Street outside the shop, turned me green with envy. The only thing that ever did make me envious was a nice sporting car or motorcycle. He first had a 14/40 Roesch Talbot close-coupled fabric-bodied Weymann sports saloon, and followed that aristocratic eyeful with one of the early Riley Kestrels, which were so streamlined and beautiful it hurt, especially if you'd got an Austin Heavy Twelve-Four or a Tin Lizzie.

I remember now you could get a haircut at the back of Tommy's shop, that was another little social centre. This came a bit later, must have been in the early 'Thirties. Before he opened up his hair-cutting parlour you had to go to old Hall's, where the decor and atmosphere in his little front parlour were strictly pre-war and the chairs hard and styling unheard-of; short-back-and-sides and that's your lot. You weren't beautifying yourself at old Hall's, you were making yourself presentable, by which was meant cropped: it was a wonderful mixture of sadism and masochism, respectively his and ours. What do you expect for four-pence, glamour?

Going up the Street was a social adventure, pretty near the only one available to all, you never knew whom you'd meet. When they knocked Pat Collins's old flea-pit cinema down and built the Grosvenor, known for years as the Groz Veener, we thought we'd never seen anything so splendid and exotic, match that Walsall. My wife's old Grandma Kinsey, who was born in Mevagissey and who wore a black bonnet and shawl, like my grandma, used to go to the matinees every time the programme changed, that is to say she went every Monday and Thursday afternoon, regular as clockwork, and strangely enough she was firmly under the impression that nobody knew. And she didn't want anybody to know. She was at chapel, the Primitive Methodists or Prims, twice every Sunday and God only knows how many times during the week, but Monday and Thursday afternoons were sacred to the secular, if I may be forgiven. Of course, with a black bonnet and shawl not to mention that Spanish-Cornish face she was fairly conspicuous and in fact everybody knew but nobody let on.

The usherettes knew her so well they put her into a ninepenny seat though she only paid fivepence. It was fivepence at the front, ninepence at the back, downstairs, but a whole shilling upstairs – and worth every penny just for the thrill of going up those glamorous winding stairs, with stunning stills in gilt frames on the walls to get you in the mood as you rose, if you needed getting in the mood. Old grandma occasionally let the cat out of the bag, of course, when junior members of the family or the congregation would be chewing the fat over the film they had seen. If they made a slip about the plot she sometimes couldn't resist putting them right. 'How do you know, grandma?' they would ask, knowing darn well how she came to know. But she never let on.

Earlier on we kids used to attend the Penny Gaff on Saturday mornings, sometimes afternoons, either at Pat Collins's flea pit or at a still older cinema on Park Side, now a factory, and even in those far-off days superannuated as a cinema and opened only once a week for the mob of kids to scream their way through old Westerns starring Tom Mix or William S. Hart. Doesn't sound like an economic proposition, especially with the pianist to pay, but there it is, it happened. Talk about bedlam! What with ordinary fights, pea-shooter marksmen, chewing gum bandits and the cigarette smoking, it was an ordeal any delicate child did well to survive.

There was a tobacconist near Belding's, not far from the corner of Church Street, where I was born, where some very curious cigarettes were displayed loose in the window, in glass vases. They were mostly stale foreign exotics, yellow, brown, faded white, some with cork tips, some with coloured tips including gold ones, some actually black. You could buy these horrors, no questions asked, singly at a halfpenny each. This was at a time when Woodbines were on sale in frail, open-ended paper packets of five, for twopence, Players cost 11½*d* for twenty and Gold Flake and most other full-size fags were a shilling the twenty pack. Criminal delinquents attending the penny gaff didn't consider themselves men unless they had one of these terrible stinking cigs. The stench was unbelievable but girls thought more of you if you smoked – though less of you if you dropped the ash off down their cleavage. It's still a matter of incredulity to me that the cinemas stood up to it, the racket, the pandemonium, the lighted matches and burning fags, the catapults and hob-nailed boots, the sheer devilry and abandon.

The surgery was another gathering place, especially for the relatively hard-up, of which there were plenty. There were several doctors who shared this establishment, which was actually not a surgery at all but a dispensary. However, it was always called the surgery. You took your prescription and waited in the most horrible dismal surroundings which the wit of man could devise – I have memories of dark green paint and dark brown lino – pervaded by those disinfectant smells – this'll teach you to be ill – and in the fullness of time your turn came and you got your bottle of jollop at the serving hatch. My old school pal Cyril Fryer worked there as a dispenser; a lovely quiet lad, he was the son of that Mr Fryer who taught me at the National School, of whom I write elsewhere.

The 'surgery' was between the Groz Veener and Philpott's the *real* tailor, no messing, superior bolts of solid cloth, wear a lifetime, cut to your measurements in what was for all you could tell to the contrary a private redbrick house. Just a discreet brass plate, Ernest Philpott, Tailor. Ernest was a very quiet, reserved man whose sister Edie married my father's brother Noah, thus becoming my Aunt Edie. Ernest was going to marry my mother's niece Beattie Smith, but she ran away with a parson instead, the Rev. Joseph Simpson Hall of blessed memory, thus giving me an honorary uncle with a manse at his disposal in which to spend heavenly holidays. Ernest never recovered from the shock, or at least he never tried again. He went to live with Noah and Edie and they lived out their quiet lives together.

The important social feature of the Street which I am unfortunately unable to discuss is the pubs. There were several, thus proving that despite our powerful nonconformist element we also had room for the usual human dissipation and bonhomie.

So strong, alas, was our teetotal tradition, in the family, that we always hurried or were hurried past these interesting establishments, and later on, when I had got a taste for the stuff and formed the habit of slipping off for a crafty half pint, I naturally avoided the boozers in the Street and frequented those in other roads. For anything that happened in the Street was public property. There was no great shortage of alternatives; you might say the place was plastered with pubs. My pals and I took our surreptitious sips in the Sir Robert Peel in Bell Lane, the Turf in Wolverhampton Road, the Spread Eagle in Leamore, or even farther afield. It's slightly sad, looking back, that of all the joys of going up the Street the one I never savoured was the one for which, in the first place, the Street was built. For undoubtedly the inn came first, the shop came second and the chapel came third. But in our time the priorities had got reversed, for historical reasons which I understand even if I don't approve.

Anyway, there it was: it was Up the Street that I first began to meet the people.

2

Enoch

UNCLE ENOCH was the most aristocratic among us. Intermarriage of dramatically different types had produced an interesting variety of physical characteristics. The generation which Uncle Enoch led comprised a perfect cross-section of the Long and the Short and the Tall, all in one family. What we like to think of as the dominant rather than the recessive characters achieved their fullest expression in Enoch, who was tall, slender, handsome and undeniably noble. He had true nobility of heart and mind, and it showed. He had a noble brow, Tennysonian hair, a carriage that was both erect and easy, a flowing way of moving and an unfailing courtesy of manner. His eyes were large, lustrous and beautiful; his voice was a joy. He also had grand ideas. This, of course, was his downfall.

It would not be too far-fetched to say that he had a Tennysonian mind. The aristocratic Celtic blood which he inherited, like the rest of us, in a more or less diffused dose, worked in the veins like an ichor, ever at war with duller, more businesslike and serviceable fluid inherited from baser though doubtless respectable sources. He had his feet firmly on the clouds and lived with panache in a romantic daydream.

Even when I was a little boy devoted to the twin and irreconcilable ideals of gallantry and compassion (split, and for ever, between pride and pity, longing for the adventurer's panache yet curdled with the conviction that holy poverty, Christian humility, were enjoined upon us by the deepest impulses of the spirit), even then I found myself lost in admiration, touched with awe, of Uncle Enoch's performance. Not that I would ever have used the word performance, or even admitted the thought. It is my loss that for half a century, despite mounting and finally irrefutable evidence to the contrary, I furiously rejected the idea that people are performers, playing out parts of their own or others' choosing.

Though I was myself continually trying on several roles for size – so wide a variety of roles that the greatest actor in the world would have failed to encompass the whole range, from cavalier to anchorite, soldier to priest, Don Juan to Savonarola, Black Prince to Saint Francis – even so I failed at first to notice, and later refused to acknowledge, that everyone else was equally intent on first recognising an attractive role and then fitting their performance to it. To admit this would have fatally impaired the romantic illusion that people were what they seemed. I could admit anything about myself, but courtesy and love alike demanded that I should not see through others' deceptions, especially self-deceptions. If I could not always turn the other cheek, I invariably turned the blind eye. All my geese were swans and I saved my reproaches for myself.

It follows that I was the last of the clan to see through Enoch's masterly performance as a tycoon to the hard core of practical incompetence within. Indeed, I can believe that even he saw through it before I did. He was perhaps the last but one to see through it. My position was firmly established in the rearguard of credulity, the ultimate straggler, the last to be converted to the asphyxiating pragmatism of common sense.

Enoch's 'failure', when it came, gave considerable pleasure to the wiseacres who had seen it coming. ('What did I tell you, eh?') In our community, which was very hot on respectability, bankruptcy was the unforgiveable sin. We need our sinners to give a spice to the bland diet of virtue, and in those far-off days before the mass media took over, when we 'had to make our own entertainment', other people's failures were the sharpest-flavoured entertainment to be had.

Needless to say, there was no lack of failures, no great shortage of objects for our censure and/or compassion, which were sometimes mingled in a bitter-sweet mix of emotions that gave an acceptable tang to the all-too-even tenor of our ricepuddingy days. Marital failures, though sometimes suspected, were rarely admitted, sexual deviations from the strict monogamous norm were few, or secret, crime in the policeman's sense was almost non-existent – confined mainly to peccadilloes of drunkenness. But financial failure was rife, and of all varieties of failure the most heinous. Actual consistent poverty was no sin – most people were poor. But if you had presumed to hoist your status well above the poverty line, to flaunt your little bit of wealth, you were as vulnerable as Icarus. You had to hang on to it, hang on like grim death, or suffer ignominy and opprobrium and pity. I fancy the sympathy was harder to bear than the scorn.

My own relations with Enoch were never intimate but always friendly, in the sense that friendship can exist between a man and a boy. More so than any of the tribe of brothers, he was cast in the same mould as my father, but on a slightly larger scale as became the eldest. Father was tall, Enoch was very tall. Father was nice-looking, Enoch was *splendid*. Father was kind, Enoch was wildly generous. Father was inclined to romanticism, Enoch was possessed by it. Father had his dreams, Enoch had nothing else.

Only now that they are all dead can I confess that of that various and remarkable family of brothers, a race apart who in one way and another left their mark on the whole community, I most liked and admired the one who fell first and farthest, who was throughout our impressionable years the standing object-lesson in how not to do it, the living warning and threat.

When he was well-off, before the fall, Enoch lived in style. It is exactly the right word. He had a sense of style and he delighted to use it. This is not the same thing as ostentation, though of course those who first envied him, then had the impertinence to pity him, were incapable of seeing the difference. It was certainly not vulgar ostentation. 'He nothing vulgar did, nor mean, Upon that memorable scene.' His worldliness had a quality of innocence. His taste was naturally good, he knew as if by instinct what suited his personality. He was not a collector, he did not accumulate *things*, but he liked to have and to use the accessories to 'gracious living' on a fairly ample and careless scale. He lived in a bigger house than anyone else in the family possessed, in the best road, for what that may have been worth, with lots of white paint on the grand staircase and balusters (at a time when most were sober brown), a large intricate and enchanting garden, and stables and a coach-house recently converted to garage. He dressed elegantly, and, as I now realise, interestingly. He was unlikely to be taken for Mayor, did not wish to be Mayor; nor yet sober-suited businessman; nor, quite, country squire. Somehow, in the dashing cut of his suits and the swirl of the brim of his soft brown trilby hat and the discreet dash and challenge of his waistcoats and ties, in the way he did not wear spats though fully entitled to, but did wear low shoes in soft brown leathers … as in the flow of his hair, the elegant briar pipe, the long well-manicured hands … I see now that he was suggesting, not wealth, not probity, not civic virtue (all of which suggestions were being made as forcefully as they knew how by the rest of the town's rising burghers) but something a whole stage beyond, something that subsumed those dreary founder virtues and made them seem provincial, elementary. What Enoch was suggesting, in his easy elegance and benevolent charm, was that opulence should generate a certain grace. He had the effrontery, which some found quite intolerable, to be an artist in the manner of his living.

It was characteristic of the man that he should drive an Overland touring car. This at a time when those of us who had graduated from push-bikes were pottering modestly around in Model T Fords and various uninspired English designs such as the Austin and the Standard. Had his prosperity continued, Enoch would doubtless have graduated from Overland to Buick, Buick to Packard. The only English cars which might have seduced him, quite possibly would have, were the Sunbeam three-litre tourer and the Vauxhall 30-98. But by the time they came along he was perforce a pedestrian.

I remember being taken by him for a ride to Walsall, in the stately yet somehow dashing and exotic Overland tourer. The hood was up, but the sidescreens were never used. We drove the three miles sedately yet with a certain swooshing and burbling *difference*, floating over the cobblestones and dodging around the occasional tram, swaying a little on the soft American springs.

Enoch removed his pipe and waved it with dignified geniality whenever we passed acquaintances, which was every few yards. If they were ladies he raised the soft brown trilby with the Tennysonian curve to its brim. Most of the way, therefore, he drove with one hand. It was perfectly feasible: he did not need one for the gear lever. The American engine, huge by our insular standards and thereby an affront to the thrifty soul of every Black Country mechanic, pulled breathily in top gear from walking pace. One day Enoch demonstrated its flexibility to an astonished and disgusted gallery by engaging gear, getting out and walking nonchalantly in front for several yards before hopping back in and accelerating down the road in a cloud of whispering haze. But he did it not so much to impress as to amuse.

When we arrived in the centre of Walsall Enoch pulled in to the kerb and told me that he wouldn't be long, he was just popping into the bank, where he had an appointment with the manager. I was deeply impressed. I knew what a bank was but did not know anyone else who used one. Most of my acquaintances managed their entire finances on the fingers of one hand, without assistance. When Enoch returned he apologised with his unfailing courtesy for being away longer than he had expected. 'The bank manager was engaged.' At these words I felt transported to a different world, a world in which people were *engaged*, people had *appointments* to consult remote stellar luminaries like bank managers (of whose functions I had not the foggiest idea). Few of the words I was hearing had any immediate meaning for me, but I sensed that this was Life with a capital L, sophisticated and mysterious beyond my dreams.

Enoch's interview with the bank manager could not have been so painful as later interviews were to be, for his mood remained sunny and expansive. He took me with him into a tobacconist-confectioner's shop, an urban emporium of staggering opulence and discretion, an Arabian Nights cavern of tasteful luxury. Here he bought an ounce of Three Nuns which he decanted into his soft leather pouch, and then he brought and presented to me a small tin of fruit pastilles. A *tin*! The glittering sugar-crusted sweets lay bedded in a couch of waxy paper within the tin: I could not bear to disturb them, but took my little tin home with me as evidence, palpable and incontrovertible, that I had visited another world. Until that moment sweets had been something the small shopkeeper scooped up with a tin trowel from naked heaps and mounds. So far as I can fix it, the year was 1919 or 1920. When I went up to Oxford in 1931 as a poor scholar I recognised, in my instant reaction to the luxurious seductive shops, their fatal insidious discretion, the same feeling of awe that I had known for the first time with Uncle Enoch on Walsall Bridge.

Three of the brothers prospered and three failed, one of them my father. His failure to make a profit as a builder, like Uncle Hiram's failure to make a profit as a farmer, were discreetly covered up by a rearguard rescue action conducted by the co-operative combined forces of the family. That is to say, there was no actual bankruptcy, no sickening public failure. When things got beyond a certain point of real insolvency, but before the bums were in, matters were 'arranged'. I have never understood how these miracles of financial diplomacy are organised. I suspect that it is largely a triumph of euphemism. We had some formidable euphemists on the sound side of the family, and some natural worriers who never had their fill of their own worries but were always ready to take on other people's. Between the two forces, a façade of unbroken rectitude and respectability was kept in repair. Whatever may have been the private reality of shame and grief, public scandal was avoided. In my father's case, the building business was quietly discontinued, the buildings and tangible assets, land and house, transferred to the original family manufacturing firm of which he and all his brothers had been member before, in 1919, three of them, flushed with the heady drug of a tiny bit of unexpected capital, broke away to set up in business on their own. My father went quietly, very quietly, back into the firm, as a paid employee, to work his way up all over again. So we escaped the stigma of bankruptcy. Of course, we were lucky. But I shall never forget the look on my father's face when he broke the news to us that his venture in freedom had come to grief.

But these were later stratagems, when we had learned the technique of the cover-up operation. Enoch had no such luck. His fall was the first and the worst, in the sense of being unmediated, public, difficult to explain away. A simple bankruptcy; it got into the papers. While my father had chosen to launch himself as a builder, and Hiram as a farmer, Enoch had chosen the leather trade, which was famous in Walsall. The streets, or some of them, reeked of tanneries. Enoch did not go into the basic side of the business, fletching and tanning, but into the prettier manufacturing side, making purses and handbags and so on. I'm afraid I don't really know much about the details. But neither did he. There must have been a pretty powerful streak of confidence in these brothers: having done well as manufacturers of metal wares, including munitions during the Great War, having risen from small beginnings to a modest but comfortable relative affluence during a generation when everything was in their favour, they must have assumed that nothing was beyond them. There was a touch of recklessness in their plunges; they were mildly heroic. But they over-estimated their virtuosity or versatility, or both. Their managerial talents were not equal to the hard times which followed the Great War. They went up like the rocket and came down like the stick.

It was a severe test of character, and they all passed it triumphantly. Character, upbringing, training and religion stood them in good stead. My father steadily worked his way up again in the old firm. He re-established his value and integrity. Working hard on the sales side, he still had time and energy to do good works. He never rested. He gave such good value to the firm that eventually he rose to be a director; all serene again. But he also found time to run his own church (he was a spiritualist) and to become a Town Councillor in the Labour interest. The poor and needy and scared and worried made a beaten track to his door. His life was full and brimming over. Hiram, having lost his farm and status of farmer, even gentleman farmer, stoically remained on the land, sweetened and supported by *his* religion (he was a Wesleyan) and true to his love for the dumb beasts and the fruitful earth. In adversity, reduced from gentleman farmer to stockman, he laboured on with unimpaired dignity and grace: never more a gentleman than then.

For Enoch, it was the end of the road. In a way, his lot was the hardest of all to bear. He was simply retired from active service. He was the eldest; he had risen farthest; he had come down fastest; there seemed nothing for him to do but retire on the wreckage of his fortune, withdraw into a dignified seclusion, living his time out in straitened circumstances, in a smaller house, a semi-detached which was at the family's disposal (one of the

first which my father had built), without a car, without an occupation, without status. He and his quiet, gentle wife had raised a
large and brilliant family, every one a character; no doubt their
love sustained him.

It was during this period that my admiration for Enoch, which
had always been touched with awe, changed to love.

Some defect in my character has always made it difficult if not
impossible for me to admire and love, wholeheartedly, people
who have made resounding successes of their lives, in the usual
meaning of the term. I suspect success, in the usual meaning of
the term. I honestly don't think there is an element of envy in
this. Brilliance, dedication and hard work are admirable, and I
can admire them: but commercial success, success in the sense
of getting on top of other people, bossy success, money-stinking
success, I have always had some reservations about. You don't
get on top of other people without wanting to, without a hard
and ruthless streak, which may be disguised even from yourself.
You don't make a fortune without loving money more than
anything or anyone else. Even in the noble field of the arts, you
don't (I suspect) come right out at the top, in terms of critical
estimation and popular success both, without a certain degree of
cunning and craftiness or at least an overweening vanity and
ambition. I find it difficult to be at ease with egocentric careerists.
Of course, there are quite a lot of egocentric failures, too, and
they can be very tiresome. But they don't frighten me like
egocentric successes.

During the whole of his retirement, when in the material sense
everything that contributed to the flowering of his personality
and life-style had been snatched away, Enoch behaved with great
dignity. He became reserved and shy, but his smile was as sweet
as ever. He was free from bitterness and envy, though he must
have had wistful regrets.

I did not see him very often. He went out very little. When I
visited him in his new home I was touched by his patience and
dignity. Sitting on the sofa before the fire, wearing a knitted
cardigan, thin-faced and rather bald now, but still with those
Tennysonian tufts of flowing hair at the sides and back, still
with those large, soft, friendly eyes, he was kind and hopeful
about *my* career. He encouraged me in that deep, vibrant voice
that used to boom out so happily, a glorious instrument. All his

advice was good, but the best advice he had to offer, though he did not know it, was his example. For it is easy to achieve success, but hard to achieve a really meritorious failure.

It was during this period that I began to see him as a Russian figure. In his palmy days, the days of the big Overland tourer and the house with the white banisters and stables and the lavish children's parties and the beautiful but slightly *outré* clothes, he was a distinctly American figure. It came to me that he had never been quite at home in the restricted ambiance of our little town. There was something, in the easy, ample *flow* of his life-style, the optimism, the spaciousness, the repudiation of strict conformity, the ready generosity, the slightly cracked romanticism – there was something here that belonged to America. Not the Western coast, not Yankee America, and not exactly the wild frontier; but the faintly absurd, attractive, doomed style of the American South. In a sense, Enoch was a Confederate gentleman. His innate aristocracy, his rectitude, his grace, his sense of style, his open-handedness combined with an effortless optimism ... he could have lived on the plantation with justice and panache.

Then, in the later period, when he sat by the fire in his cardigan, with his long big-knuckled hands folded over an empty pipe, listening with exquisite attention to the rattlings of smaller souls who had not been beaten, he was still a foreign and exotic figure, but now from a different scene. As I began to read the Russian authors I began to recognise him all over again, as a figure from Chekov or even Gogol. Not quite Uncle Vanya and not quite Chebutykin – he had some of Chebutykin's gentle resignation but none of his ultimate cynicism. There were even hints of him in Dostoievsky and Gorki.

Of course Enoch was unaware of this. He was a midland man of mixed descent with a strong Celtic and aristocratic streak, imprisoned in a small village-town on the rim of the Black Country, a commercial failure with a fondness for Tennysonian eloquence and rhetoric and a sound grounding in the hymns of Wesley and the unforgiving edicts of nonconformity. He lived out his whole life there, rising to a peak of flowering brilliance and ending almost meek.

I have always wished that I had been less shy and had talked to him more freely. I think he would have been touched to know how often I thought of him and how deeply his life was to influence my own. Touched and amazed.

He was born a hundred years ago. His father, my grandfather, whom I knew well, was born before the Crimean War, and *his* father was alive at the time of Trafalgar and Waterloo. I do not feel so much a parvenu on this earth when I think of this ancestry. It is as if I can almost stretch out my hand and touch a kinsman who wore buckskin breeches and a beaver hat and had fought in the Peninsular Wars; and hear his voice as a familiar. Strangely enough, Enoch, not my own father, is my link with a certain aspect of my lineage, which is so mixed. I never really knew him very well. But he lives on in my memory.

3

Billy and Chink

WHEN I was a little boy, too young for school, we lived near the Pinfold. The *Oxford English Dictionary* tells us that pinfold from the Old English *pundfald* means 'a place for confining stray or distrained cattle, etc.; a pound; later, a fold for sheep, cattle, etc'. In our time it was getting to be a bit built-up, or built-around, with a factory or two, small and greater Victorian houses and even earlier slums, all black with grime, a few shops and the Primitive Methodist chapel. But there was still a small farm operating at the Pinfold, run by Mr Holyman whose sons and daughter all went to Oxford; I have been in the byre in the evening, as an infant during the Great War, waiting while the cows were milked by lamplight. And there was still a bit of ragged, tummocky meadow, with a little pool, where beasts grazed and ran. And through the main artery ran the single-line tram track. The trams came groaning up the gradient from Leamore, past the Spread Eagle and the Lamp Tavern and our factory which was also our home, snaking and rocking round the S-bend of the Pinfold proper at the top of the rise, past Doctor Drabble's house where Philip Drabble was born, then accelerating away on the cobbles, rocking and clanging, past the chapel and Billy's repair shop, towards Bloxwich proper, the Street.

Between Billy's repair shop and our house there were a few rather come-down Victorian houses, which had been fairly grand; one of them was a private school called Teddesley House, thought to be very posh; and then a row of terribly poor cottages, tucked away behind the houses that fronted the main road, at a slight angle; blackened redbrick little houses with no conveniences at all, swarming with children and oddities.

In this row lived Chink. I can give him no other name because I never heard that he had one; though he must have done, it must have been registered somewhere. But there was a great deal less bureaucracy then. Chink was our simpleton. He was terribly deformed. His body was warped and his mind was in a permanent infancy. He made noises but I am not sure that he could truly speak. To a few, he was a figure of fun; to many, a figure of unspeakable pathos; to some, a terrible apparition.

Chink moved freely among us. Nothing official was done to him, for him, or against him. I find it often difficult to realise how little 'official' life there was when I was a boy. There was some, of course; we were not living in original Eden; there were laws to be obeyed or disregarded, there were policemen and teachers and Town Councillors, and somewhere in the distance there was a Government, utterly remote and unthought-of except at election times; if then. But there was virtually no official 'welfare'. Private charity, private medicine, private enterprise were still the rule. The school attendance officer would seek you out if you played the wag, but that was about as far as it went. Out of school hours, and after your schooldays, you were very much on your own, you and your friends and your enemies, and your family. You sank or swam, mucked in together or fell out; neither way did the State take very much interest. It was your life to spoil or celebrate.

If you had a child like Chink, now.... Well, it would be illegal to kill him, of course, though you could hear compassionate ones with hard fronts murmur, 'He'd be better off out of his misery' and even 'Ought to have been drowned at birth'. But apart from being required by law not actually to murder him, you were quite at liberty to bring him up as you thought fit. It was your problem. There was no one to turn to, no help to be had. If he turned violent, ah, well, now, that's another matter, you can have him put away if he's a danger to life and property. But if he turns out as Chink turned out, just useless, daft, ugly, misshapen, harmless and hopeless. . . . Hard luck, missus, do the best you can.

So Chink just wandered around. His poor body was a living wreck, he lurched and staggered, flailing the air wildly with his single crutch, which was no more than a worn-out, bristle-free broom cut down to size. He literally looked just like a scarecrow in the fields, he wore a battered old top hat like a clown's, and his face was the sort of face children paint on their guy around Bonfire Night: staring, distorted, surrealist; slavering pink gash of mouth; slanting eyes that gave him his cruel name, Chink. This was a time when a dark-skinned man was a nigger, an oriental was a chink, a white foreigner of any culture or lineage was a dago or a wop. We were insular, we were ignorant, we were suspicious and proud. We had been taught from childhood, whatever else we might have been taught, that Britain ruled the waves and that wogs began at Calais. You can't blame us: that is how it was.

But Chink didn't wander around the straggling village-town being insulted, jeered-at, hooted and stoned—as he might possibly have been, a century earlier. There were just those few children who mocked him and taunted him, of course there were, he was a natural grotesque target for the spleen and venom of those who felt inadequate and visited their rage on anything outlandish. And there are always naturally cruel people around, naturally nasty. But by and large and in a general sort of way, Chink was *tolerated*. It's a funny word to use; I can see how it might give rise to misunderstandings. I'm not trying to suggest, smugly, that there was anything fine and noble in people *tolerating* the poor devil; it sounds like condescension. What I'm trying to say is that whereas nowadays the Chinks of this world (or at any rate this country) are shut away in very kind places where very kind people work very hard to make them happy, in those old days Chink was just chucked out to sink or swim on the general surface of society. You could see him around, in fact you couldn't miss him, he wasn't shut away out of sight and he wasn't made the special out-of-sight responsibility of kind specialists: no, he was just there, on view, everybody had to accept him for what he was and do whatever one thought it best to do. He was all sorts of things to all sorts of people and to various sections inside individual people: he was a reproach, a reminder, a rebuke, a fright, a terrible joke, an object of pity, a nuisance, or whatever he was. He was whatever you thought he was, and whatever you thought he was defined you, too.

He wasn't usually naughty, though once when I was tiny I saw him leap in front of a tram belting down the single track on the cobbles outside our house. The driver slammed the emergency brake on and the tram screamed to a stop, rocking and shuddering, people jumping up and crying out. The driver got out, white as a sheet as everyone said, and gave Chink a terrific tongue-lashing. Chink was laughing in a slavering sort of way, more horrible to behold than most people's tears. He hadn't been trying to end it all (as well he might have): it was just devilment, even a child could see that, everybody agreed it was just devilment. The driver was shaken, in fact everybody was shaken, including me; I hadn't seen such drama before. Only Chink was unshaken. Nothing was 'done about it': it was just an incident, nearly a 'serious' incident; now it was all over, life went on, everyone went about their business. It was the only incident I knew of or heard of in which Chink figured as a *wilful* nuisance: normally – what a word! – normally he was just an involuntary nuisance, human litter, something that people wished weren't there but put up with with what compassion they had. And some of them had quite a lot. Girls and girl children and old ladies and even young ladies didn't much like having Chink suddenly appear, lurching out of an alley in front of them, grinning and gasping. He gave them the shudders. But so far as I could tell, most people just, well, as I was saying, just tolerated him. He was somebody's hard luck, and in a small sense he was everybody's hard luck. But we hadn't yet reached that point in our social development where we segregated our bits of hard luck. We let them live their lives out, among us, not exactly taking part in the usual run of living, because they couldn't, but at any rate not excluded from it; free to hang around and look on and even pretend to participate. My God, it was rough but was it so entirely contemptible? We attempted no cure, no systematic amelioration: but neither did we have it swept away, hidden. I mean we were human: we hadn't bureaucratised ourselves frozen. Yet. And another thing you have to bear in mind: a lot of people could actually bring themselves to believe that they were as badly off as Chink, or even worse off. There were a lot of war widows and orphans, more every day, and they had the wits to comprehend their loss.

Billy came back from the war and I think he resumed his old occupation as chauffeur-mechanic to Doctor Mac. I'm pretty sure I remember seeing him driving the doctor about in a yellow Standard two-seater with artillery wheels and a Cape Cart hood, as he had done before the war. But whether I'm truly remembering this, or whether I'm just remembering the snapshot which I certainly have seen, the fact is that Billy did not go on being Doctor Mac's chauffeur for any great length of time after the end of the war, and that may well be because Doctor Mac died, as die he certainly did, not long after doctoring my broken nose. At any rate, Billy opened a repair shop on the Pinfold, nominally dealing with motorcycle and bicycle repairs, and it was at this point that the lines of his life and the life of Chink began to converge.

My wife still has fading snapshots and postcards which Billy sent to her from the Western Front. I'm just looking at a card which says on the back, in pencil, 'From Mons'. He used to send her little presents, and he always sent her his love. He always told her she was his sweetheart. You see, Billy lived next door to this little girl, who also lived near the Pinfold. There are so many strings and strands of my life that wind back in a tangle to the Pinfold, though we left there when I was four. But I kept going back, I keep going back, shall I ever be free?

Billy's little business was not a success. I don't know that it was ever meant to be a 'success'. It was to be a living, of course, but it was also a way of life. It's a very delicate equation; it can easily tremble into a fatal disequilibrium. It depends on which you *really* value most, in your secret heart – the living or the way of life.

I think Billy valued the way of life. Of course I could be wildly wrong, but we are entitled to form our judgments, make our guesses. From what I know of Billy and from what I saw of the business, I'd say he wasn't much interested in making a profit but deeply, deeply interested in the way of life.

Think of it. Chauffeur-mechanic to Doctor Mac, a superior servant; then the years in Flanders, *those* dreams; then the sudden possibility opening up – his own business, his own master: free, alive, whole in body and mind, a survivor and a free man. I for one can well believe that to Billy, the way of life meant more than the living.

In many ways Billy epitomised the essential Black Country man. He was not very tall, but sturdy, stocky: we had a phrase, more admiring than diminishing, 'a little stiff 'un'. It was said of growing boys, appreciatively: ' 'E's gooin' to be a little stiff 'un, eh?' I can't recall if there was a complementary phrase for tall thin gangling chaps, of the 'stick of macaroni' or 'streak of cold water' kind. Billy was a typical Black Country little stiff 'un. He was also a very quiet man, even quieter than the usual run, and on the whole we were quiet people, more preached against than preaching. He was dark, rounded rather than square; almost pudgy; I can see his strong pudgy hands. And he was a born potterer, as so many of the men I remember from childhood were. Pottering is a way of life in itself.

Billy was a good mechanic, if not very good. He made up some remarkable bikes out of odd pieces. There was perhaps a touch of hopeless romance and poetry in his fitting. He came of mechanic stock; his father, old man Ison, was a file sharpener. In those days, when factories used a great deal of hand work, a man could make a living sharpening their files. The old man sharpened all Wilkcs's files, I believe, and he may have sharpened ours. His front parlour was full of files. There was no room in it for anything else. In a shed in his back yard he preserved a real antique of a horse-drawn carriage, dating back, it was believed, to Queen Victoria's coronation time. My wife and her little pals used to play grandly imaginative games in it. So perhaps Billy inherited both his mechanical flair and his tendency to hoard mechanical junk from old man Ison.

You might say that his lifework consisted of gathering mechanical junk around him. Some people find the detritus of cast-off machinery deeply depressing and ugly; others find it actually beautiful, appealing, magnetic, and surround themselves with it, becoming submerged in stuff all of which has or is believed to have a problematic or potential utility. 'It may come in handy' is their wistful gospel. Of such was Billy.

He accumulated imperfect and incomplete machinery, spares, bits and pieces. At first he actually travelled around to find it, in his motorcycle combination with the wickerwork sidecar, and later in his own little two-seater Standard. But he did not have to travel for long. People soon realised that Billy could not say no to an obsolete three-speed hub, a crankcase with the timing cover missing, a petrol tank, a pair of forks, a wheel for which no tyre would ever be made again. The stuff accumulated, spilling out from his little shop on to the pavement, which happened to be very wide just at that point – there was no 'town planning' in those days, you built as you thought fit. Quite soon Billy had an extensive stock of items which were difficult to obtain, partly because few enough customers wished to obtain them. As his collection grew – it seems more accurate to call it his collection, rather than his stock—so Billy seemed to grow into it, as a shepherd sometimes seems to grow into his flock or a very keen eccentric gardener grows into his greenhouse plants or his trees and shrubs. You've seen pet shop proprietors who are almost indistinguishable from their pets? So it was with Billy. He had created his perfect milieu. He pottered ceaselessly, never moving fast, picking over his stuff and moving things slightly. For long periods he just stood and looked at it.

But Billy could still have prospered in a small way; he had stuff which *somebody* wanted (and could find nowhere else) and he had his skills. But he had also a crushing fault in a business man. He had a soft heart. People came to know this and they preyed upon him. At the best of times Billy found it difficult to name 'a sensible price'. Knowing what he had paid for it, he could not, I mean literally, could not bring himself to ask much more for it than he had given. There are people like this. Billy's soft-heartedness would be bad enough in a man who did not have a business to run; in a businessman, it was disastrous. 'He'd give you his heart,' people said. In fact he was perpetually giving his heart. You received a portion of that oversize organ with every purchase you made.

For a time Billy managed to keep ticking over. A very small profit was enough to satisfy him. The young woman whom he courted for years eventually gave him up, in despair of ever making him see commercial sense. A bachelor, and growing older and more isolated, more on his own, he needed little enough. But there were too many who saw him as a nest that just had to be robbed, a hive that simply had to be raided. Billy 'began to go downhill'.

As the bright hopes of the 'Twenties faded, as the cosy dream of his own business, his own home with his own wife and family imperceptibly faded out of his life like a dye that was not fast, so Billy withdrew from that happy 'normality' which was not to be fully realised. It was a very gradual process. As middle age slipped into old age, as his resources dwindled and even the supply of scroungers and spongers dried up, Billy turned his mansuetude and his boundless charity upon the one human object that was still not too proud to receive it.

Chink had always been fascinated by Billy's junk. And in Billy he found a refuge and a protector. Here was a normal man who would never take advantage of his abnormality, never tease and never turn him away. Chink's presence at the shop was never good for trade, but to Billy, humanity was more important than machinery, much as he loved machines.

In a way that would absolutely not have been predictable, on that day when Chink stepped in front of the tram, while Billy was in Flanders writing gay brief love letters to a little girl, with the bright future all before him ... the strange lines of fate or destiny or design came wavering together, clinched and cohered in a human partnership which words cannot describe, but only hint at.

The last I heard, and that was many years ago, all trace of Billy's business enterprise had long been swept away, he was looking after Chink in a poor lodging in the town. No one would ever have imagined these two lives ending in this pattern. No one would have had the right.

I do not have enough information of the documentary sort to sketch in those last years. But you can imagine for yourself. Someone had to hold the poor wretch's hand as everything went dark and sour and the night of life set in. Someone who could not care enough about making a profit, but could not live without caring. Someone who knew that in the end the only loss is loneliness, the only profit is love.

4

A Gentleman

ALMOST opposite our house in Lichfield Road there lived a gentleman. We will call him Mr Major. He may indeed have held military rank, though when I became aware of him, during the Great War of 1914-1918, he was long past military age. But he may have served in the Sudan, or perhaps in Afghanistan. He looked the part perfectly.

He was a tall, erect old chap with silver hair and a beautiful white military moustache. His cheeks were pink, his back was straight and he walked with just a touch of swagger. Three things proved him a gentleman. He spoke like one and he dressed as we believed a gentleman should dress. In addition, he did not work. He was a man of independent means.

Every morning he left the house and walked along Lichfield Road and up past the Park to The Street, wearing a silver-grey Homburg hat, a blue melton overcoat, pin-striped trousers and spats. He carried a silver-headed walking cane and he wore lavender-coloured gloves. When he passed a woman with whom he was acquainted, he treated her as a lady, raising his hat and making a slight bow. When he passed a boy, whether acquainted or not, he waved or twirled his walking cane in a genial yet faintly menacing way.

Once a week, in the morning at about eleven, he went up to Arch's shop, known as the Dairy, and bought a Madeira cake. He carried it back on the flat of his left hand, balancing it as a waiter balances a plate. Something about this delicate balancing act served to emphasise his air of distinction. Anyone else would grasp the paper bag by the top and swing it; or tuck it under his arm. But Mr Major carried it home in a manner which suggested that he knew quite well that an officer and a gentleman should really not be expected to carry parcels, but circumstances, you know, circumstances.... And in the circumstances, he was making the best of a bad job in a perfectly honourable way. He wasn't trying to disguise the slight element of comedown, he wasn't pretending that he wasn't carrying a cake home, he was proffering it to the world in a delicate yet somehow manly way that said, See here, good people, I'm not really used to this kind of chore, but you will observe that I do what must be done with a bit of an air, and without quite soiling my hands.

I never heard anyone say a bad word about Mr Major. Not an actual bad word. He was much respected for his gentlemanliness, and although the Majors 'kept themselves to themselves' it was generally understood that this was not from standoffishness but because, living in reduced circumstances, they could not afford to become involved in the cheerful gregariousness and endless reciprocated hospitality – even if it amounted to no more than cups of tea – which went on all around them.

I know that it was a Madeira cake that Mr Major bought at Arch's the Dairy because one day I asked him outright what he had got in the paper bag. He was courtesy personified. He explained to the impudent small boy and even went so far as to open the bag and show me the soft brown top of the cake incrusted with a sliver of lemon peel. He went further, and told me about the place called Madeira and the wine that came therefrom. I had not heard of wine – ours was a regrettably teetotal household – and when I got home I asked to be enlightened. All I got was the temperance lecture and a scolding for asking Mr Major 'personal questions'. This was the first time I had come across the phrase *personal questions*, the first time I heard of wine, and very nearly if not quite the first time I got a whiff of social distinctions.

We left Lichfield Road quite soon thereafter and I never saw Mr Major again. But he remained in my mind as the archetypal representative of a different sort of human being. 'Our sort' were busy, bustling, hard-working toilers in the vineyard, getting on, rising in the world, cheerful, tea-swigging, teetotal, Wesleyan, hymn-singing, emotional, democratic – well, Liberal – devoted to making money and getting educated, really late-Victorian in our ethos and as lively as the yeast in the dough. Mr Major belonged to another part of the forest. Professional people, not too well off, C. of E., wearing pin-stripe trousers, spats and Homburg hats.... I just about got the message that we looked down in a genial and not really unkind way on his straitened means; laughed quietly at his old-world habits and manners; and ever so slightly envied him his unchallengable distinction. None of this was ever laid out explicitly to be learned by rote. I just got the impression. Little boys and girls can be crafty animals with sensitive antennae.

'Ain't got two ha'pennies to rub together' was the usual remark about people with more pretensions than were considered becoming.

We, of course, had got two ha'pennies to rub together. And were always rubbing them.

5

Horace

HORACE was a grown man of twenty-six and I was a boy of ten when first we met. But there was never a gap between us. He came to court my sister, who was seven years older than me, and he was therefore nine years older than she was. My parents were in their very early forties, so they were as much older than Horace as Horace was older than me. I mention these figures because in a strange and soothing way Horace was everybody's contemporary. He had that rare total naturalness which made age seem unimportant, in fact unnoticeable. There was never any need to 'change gear' with him – he was exactly the same person when talking to me, to people of his own age, or to my parents. Or to anybody. He was absolutely his own fresh natural self, without a trace of subterfuge or artificiality, and his nature was full of love. He was one of those 'holy simpletons' of Dostoievsky. Blake would have recognised him instantly as a holy simpleton.

Horace came into our lives through a shared interest in spiritualism. The spiritualism came into his life before my sister, if you follow me. Both interests were sincere. Horace had no insincere interests. In the year 1922 people came from far and wide to taste this new experience, spiritualism; which, so far as our parish was concerned, had just been invented, and mainly by my father. My parents took a lease on a derelict shop and turned it into the first spiritualist temple in the district, and Horace was one of the many who came by pushbike, pony and trap, milk float, two-stroke, four-stroke, tram, bus, brake and Shanks's Pony, from hamlets as far afield as New Invention to the West, Landywood to the North, and Leamore to the South, to hear the Word preached and to see the new spells cast. I do not recollect that any pilgrims came from the East, nor Wise Men either. But hazard no guess as to why.

At this stage in the history of the world – of which after all he was a part, his doings an integral factor – Horace was running a lamp-oil round from Rushall, where he lived. Daily he set off from the family shop with a shaggy old pony harnessed in the shafts of a pre-war float, laden with paraffin which he sold by the gallon and the quart to cottage dwellers for miles around who had not yet been granted the boon of electricity.

It may not seem very much of a career, but you have to bear in mind that many people's jobs were still less attractive, and by a considerable margin. Assuming that they *had* jobs; a large assumption. It was an occupation which kept him on the move, in the fresh air. It brought him into daily contact with a lot of people, with all of whom he formed a sort of friendship. And it compared very favourably with his previous occupation, war.

For Horace was one of the citizen soldiers of that New Army, known otherwise as Kitchener's Army, which fought the Germans to a standstill in the mud of Passchendaele, the Ypres Salient, and the battlefields astride the Somme. He was a boy barely twenty on the morning of the First of June, 1916, when the New Divisions walked over towards the enemy lines after the greatest barrage in history, expecting to find all the Germans dazed or dead – and found them very much alive, protected by deep fortifications from which, in considerable security, they emerged to massacre the advancing British. Horace fought also in the Battle of Arras, in Third Ypres, and at Passchendaele. He did not himself deal out death on a personal basis to any German, being a signaller, who spent many a lonely hour crouched in sap and shell-hole trying to make the rudimentary telephones and telegraphs of the time pass back their awful messages. He took a pride – a very quiet pride – in the fact that he had shot no man. But he was there to be shot at. And it left its mark.

Not in the form of neurasthenia, which, in many a subtle disguise, changed the lives of so many survivors. He was a very brave young man to whom all life was naturally a risk, and his nerves were not impaired by experiences which broke some nervous systems even when the physical body escaped whole. But the mark which war left on Horace was subtler still and harder to distinguish, unless you looked very closely. It took the form of a total heart-sickness with the system that allowed and encouraged men to behave so badly to one another. Underlying his native unspoiled sweetness of nature, which nothing ever destroyed, underlying his overflowing love for humanity and his ready belief in human goodness, there lay this disgust, too deep for tears, with the aggressive society. It did not often show itself explicitly, though it was always behind every loving gesture and unselfconscious courtesy: but when it flared up, when it burst out in words and behaviour, it was painful, to many, in proportion as it was surprising, coming from so quiet a young man.

I had many friends of my own age, some of whom I loved dearly, some of whom I loved to hate, secretly but with passion. I think this may be more normal than is usually allowed. I was not solitary, even in my fantasies; one or two congenial friends had fantasies as extravagant and peculiar as my own. And then there was the usual crowd of contemporaries whom one never really knew at all, but who passed for friends, in the sense that they kept one company, shared or were believed to share some of the same interests, did not actively show detestation. Yet with all this wealth of company, some of it congenial, I always 'had time' for Horace, and he for me. Almost all adults were by definition untrustworthy, foreign and intensely boring; Horace had, as I say, this unique distinction of being everyone's contemporary. He was entirely welcome in all our pursuits and plans: we kept no secrets from him. Of course he sometimes disapproved of our absurdities, but he expressed his disagreement in terms which one could accept, which never alienated us. His advice was frequently taken. If sometimes he got us into scrapes, he oftener got us out.

During childhood one naturally never defined the terms of this curious relationship. It was enough that it existed. Horace shared

many activities, though he never took to fishing. One's inter-
mittent effort to become fit and strong, an athlete, he abetted
with enthusiasm; alas, I never had the staying power for all that
dreary training, though there were times when this most unlikely
ambition took some sort of grip on the capricious imagination
and long runs, sparring and wrestling, cricket and football seemed
actually interesting and important. But one never persevered, in
anything, except the resolution which set like concrete in childhood, to become a writer. And even that was to be side-tracked
– perhaps it was just as well – by the seductive and meretricious
attractions of journalism.

As one grew up it became impossible to ignore the fact that
Horace, though universally liked, was not universally respected
by the older generation. They saw him as ineffectual. It became
obvious that he was unlikely to win any of life's glittering prizes.
The point being that he did not prize them. We were now moving,
uneasily and uncertainly, into that period in the family's
corporate life when we had to face the fact that other families
were cleverer and richer. We were becoming aware that outside
the close-knit family circle there was a wider world, and it was
tough. A world in which the little Wiggins' inborn conviction that
there couldn't be a family nicer than themselves carried no
weight. We had been brought up in some comfort and in the
assurance that there was always a refuge in the bosom of the
ever-loving family. We had been spoiled by love. Little by little,
as the terrible 'Twenties rolled by and the Great Depression
loomed up, we began to cotton on to the essential nastiness of
life, the cruelty of the aggressive society. Father was struggling
to make a go of his building business – later he had to confess
himself beaten and go back into the family firm, a refuge but
not without its thorns. Money was tight. We were better-off than
many if not most of our friends, but still keenly aware of the
precariousness of commercial life, the ever-present possibilities
of disaster. I do not mean that we brooded over it, but we were
no longer innocent.

Horace's socialism, which was of a primitive Christian kind,
became paradoxically an embarrassment. There were few willing
to deny it in principle. On the other hand, it was plainly impera-
tive to strike out on one's own and seize a piece of the cake. The
conflict between the wish to gain security – not wealth: just

security, however modest – and the wish to alter the ghastly system in favour of everyone having a better share of the crumbling cake, led to some heart-searchings. It was one thing to be as sweet-natured and lovable as Jesus, it was quite another to be so obviously incapable of making enough money to support one's daughter in the manner to which she was accustomed. It was really an awful paradox, most painful. I saw how it appeared to my parents. They couldn't have wanted a nicer guy than Horace for a son-in-law, but on the other hand they couldn't help wishing he'd been rich with it.

Given Horace's temperament and convictions, there was never the faintest chance that he would grow rich. There seemed precious little chance that he would ever make enough to marry on. To compound the paradox, my sister was going to be a teacher, earning as much as £4 a week – this at a time when fathers of families were managing on thirty bob. And total security with it, respectability beyond question, long holidays. . . . How could she throw herself away on a chap who couldn't earn £4 a week regularly if he stood on his head? Oh, it was painful, painful.

The central fact was that Horace did not give a damn for money. He did not value the 'right things'. What he had he gave away; he was the softest touch I ever knew, and I say this in the light of sixty years of experience of being a pretty soft touch myself. His Christianity was of that primitive sort which accepts that we should 'take no thought for the morrow'. The Lord will provide. And I suppose the Lord did, after a fashion; or somebody did, for I must tell you they eventually married and lived happily ever after, or at least until Horace's death at the age of sixty. It wasn't that he wouldn't work – he was a most diligent and assiduous worker, he loved to work. It was simply that he couldn't or wouldn't 'look after himself', as the phrase went. 'Look after Number One.' He would not demean himself to look after Number One. He worked, incongruously, as some sort of under-manager in various factories, looking after everybody else and accepting whatever the management chose to give him, for himself. He worked as a salesman and a demonstrator (he was happy at this, in Woolworth's: he enjoyed the company). He worked at anything.

He shouldn't have been working in a factory, or as a salesman;

he should have been teaching or preaching. He was the incarnation of the self-educated man, the perfect product of the Forster
Education Act of 1870 which gave everyone compulsory education up to a certain minimal elementary standard and then threw
the vast majority of them on the scrapheap of industrial society,
just when their appetites were whetted for something a bit better.

Horace read voraciously, buying books from the penny box
which in those days stood outside every bookshop – and sometimes
the twopenny and the sixpenny boxes, too; sometimes spending
money he hardly owned on costlier books. What he read he did
not invariably digest, but that is true of most readers. We need
to be taught to read. He was crammed with half-digested information and, especially, with misunderstood or imperfectly understood philosophy and metaphysics. Like me, he was a sucker
for philosophy and metaphysics. We enjoyed poetry and were
forever reciting it, by the yard, to anyone who would listen and
doubtless to many who would have preferred not to. But our
staple drug, the one we were hooked on, was philosophy. There
are few more dangerous.

In this sense, as in others, Horace made a contribution to my
education the consequences of which were more far-reaching
than anyone realised; including myself. As I grew from a boy into
a youth I became strangely clear-sighted about other people's
mental abilities, though not always about their hearts. I could
be taken in, and frequently was, by people who professed friendship, or even enmity. I tended to take their emotions at face
value. But I was rarely misled about their brains. I knew well
enough the limitations of my own brain power. I gauged my
intelligence pretty shrewdly, and realised that I was intuitive
rather than intellectual. I had just enough intellectual power to
be able to distinguish the calibre of other intellects. And I knew
that Horace was not a powerful thinker. He was confused in the
way that self-educated men can be. Yet, I say, he had a far-
reaching effect on my education. Not by what he taught me, for
he taught me very little in the strict or bookish sense; but by
what he allowed me to infer about the reality as opposed to the
appearances of human intercourse.

After knowing Horace intimately for a decade, while I grew
from boy to man, I had no illusions left about the injustice of life,
the gulf between appearance and reality. I continued for many

years to give a fair imitation of a man who has not made that
discovery, hoping always to be re-converted back into a state of
innocence. But I knew. I knew perfectly well that to them that
hath, shall it be given, and from them that hath not, it shall be
taken away, even that which they have. I had absorbed his belief,
his passionate conviction, that success is a vulgar impostor. One
goes one way or the other. On receiving this intimation of the
non-justice of human affairs, one becomes either a cynical go-
getter, determined to do the other man before he does you; or
one becomes *disgusted*, a drop-out, a non-joiner, wholly disillu-
sioned by the vulgarity of material success and determined only
never to be seduced by it. Of course one wavers between poles –
total consistency is not on – but by and large, that was the general
cast of my thinking and feeling throughout the formative phases
of my commercial adult life. I did quite well, in fact, having a
natural aptitude for some aspects of the business which I entered.
But not nearly so well as I might have done had I not, from the
start, been flawed by the conviction that the rat race was for
rats.

This is what I gained from my lifelong friendship with my
brother-in-law Horace.

True, I did not for long share his Christianity. I did not actually
argue with him about it, but quietly dropped out when the conflict
between pretension and performance became too much.

YES, but what was he actually *like*? Come out from behind
these abstractions, I hear you say; your philosophising bores me,
I yawn over your earnestness. What was the man *like*? How did
you pass the time?

He was rather below the average height, but well built, with
a developed torso and quite muscular arms and legs. His colouring was fair. His cheeks were pink, his hair golden and very fine
in texture. His eyes were a beautiful clear blue, the very hue of
innocence. The skin of his body was as smooth and silky as a
fair woman's. He had poor teeth and a weak chin. All the planes
of his face receded. It was not strong. He wore wire-rimmed
glasses, gold in colour, which were always in need of a good
breathy wipe. He was in too much of a hurry to catch up on the
dream to bother much about things like polishing glasses or
shoes. He was fastidiously clean in his person, but he couldn't

be bothered about clothes and such, though he took a childish delight in a new jacket, say. But it didn't stay new long. He wore baggy flannel trousers and tweed jackets and his tie was carelessly knotted and his collar often crumpled.

He was always in a hurry to catch up on the dream.

This made him a good companion for people who were equally besotted with a foolish notion of reality behind appearances. The ability to ignore circumstances, literally not to believe the evidence of your eyes; to walk about in a world that was not there, but should have been. . . . He hadn't yet heard that 'the surface of things *is* the heart of things'. He could enter into childish games like cowboys and Indians, but better and by far were the games which were not explicitly acknowledged to be games, the scripts which we acted out as we made them up, going along, making use of whatever props reality put there to be used, plays in which everyone else had a walking-on part, or even a speaking part, yet were minor characters, to be coped with, circumvented as all awkward realities were to be circumvented: the plays in which we starred. Joint starring roles, you under-stand; the role of hero. We both wrote appalling poetry, to be read aloud, walking along the canal bank or over the ravaged moorland laid waste by a century of mining, mining and sub-sidence, earth-grabbing, foundries and blast furnaces, pitheads, shafts, levels, sinkings, the quays and canals and the jewelled reed-fringed pools as deep as night; slagheaps, mountains in miniature of shale and slag and waste, tips, level crossings, signal boxes, bridges, deep sunken lanes between mountains of slag, viridian green grass growing round tiny pools; waste land slimy with the detritus of a century of indifferent greed, exploita-tion, cruelty and heroism, suffering, accident, blast, fire-damp, explosion. . . .

O corduroy-trousered heroes of my boyhood, where are you now? Dead, forgotten, no, never forgotten, live again, dear pallid heroes of the undernight, the underday, the galleries and stinking shafts. Sulphurous air. Snap-boxes. Trousers of moleskin or hard corduroy, tied beneath the knee with string or strap. White eye-balls staring out of black faces, pink nigger-lips. Nigger minstrels, singing homewards, not loud, not the Welsh *hwyl*, but throaty dirges, sardonic-sentimental mockery. . . . *Brave boys*, your king and country need you, the pointing finger and popping eyes and lurid mad moustache of the great homosexual field marshal, Lord Kitchener of Khartoum, eating babes for breakfast they say the Germans are, go and fight dear lad, your king and country need you and brave little Belgium needs you; then back to the under-lay and undernight, little puffers puffing across the wasteland between the pitheads, D. H. Lawrence country, who? never heard of him, shuffle across the level crossing, wave the red flag. Dark below, and pigeons waiting uppersides in their hutches, their lofts made of all manner of scrap timber lifted, begged, borrowed, bits of wire netting. Gotta feed the pigeons first. The waif dogs, *O lurcher-loving collier, black as night,* that's Auden you know, O lurcher-loving collier black as night. Prisoners on parole tramp-ing home the five miles, heavy boots ringing off the metalled road, nigger lips, staring white eyes in black faces, O Christ O Christy minstrels.

Grey-ochre, viridian jewels, impasto of slimy grey with rust-red rails, streaked with the black dead black of the pit heads, the railway bridge always black in any light, oblique it crossed the cut, the cut oblique it cut across the ravaged landscape, cut our bursting hearts. I say they left their hearts behind in Flanders field, poppy-blown, can you see a poppy now and not weep, Horatio? Weep, Horatio, Horatio, there are more things in heaven and earth than are dreamt of in thy philosophy, Horatio. They say there were rats in the trenches as big as cats, so cool so fat they fed calmly on the dross the bullets left behind. Rats here, too, we hunted them when we were boys, a boyo sport, hunted with terriers sticks and bricks, no mercy for the rat. The rat on two legs, Horatio, the rat behind the Arras ... We never caught up with *him.* Not *that* one. He escaped.

You see we were idiots, we didn't know which side our bread was buttered, we didn't give three of a dog's whether 'twas buttered or bare. Dry bread of charity, Horace said often to me, when we were away walking the ravaged landscape, dry bread of charity, Sam, it sticks in the gullet.

My middle name is Sam and old friends still use it.

He was fierce about charity. Said it stuck in the throat.

'I managed on ten bob last week,' he said once. He was sitting in the old granfeyther chur by the kitchen fire, the blackleaded range. Once when we'd been cleaning something off my trousers with a drop of petrol in a cocoa tin, a speck or two of tar I expect

it was, I threw the last drop of petrol on the back of the fire to
see what would happen. They said I should come to no good. But
did you really and truly, did you honest, cross your heart, did you
want to come to good if it's like this, poor beggars on the dole,
working three shifts, two shifts a wik, for ten bob a shift?

A grown man in business on his own account, well, in the
family business, anyway, with a lamp-oil round of his own,
working out in all weathers five and sometimes six days a wik,
fust light to what, six at night sometimes, then the pony to be
bedded down and fed. Ten bob he took out of the takings for
himself, that's bacca, matches, tram fares, the bit in the plate, the
coppers for the kids, the papers you like to read, still half-
believing, the *New Statesman and Nation,* now *that's* the paper,
Sam, the *Daily Herald,* the *Two Worlds* edited by Maurice
Barbanell, Sir Oliver Lodge was a spiritualist, you know, don't
mock, Sam, reserve your judgment if you like but don't mock,
there's more things in heaven and earth than dreamt of in thy
philosophy, Horatio.

Ten bob a week for a grown man. To *manage* on. I had
nightmares. There was this point at which the indifferent callous-
ness of the grown-up world.... You can't expect to understand
everything, Sam, it takes time, better brains than us have been
trying for centuries.

Shelley was his favourite poet. Reciting Shelley by the yard,
walking the tips and the cut bank. The poet of rebellion and
liberty. Trying to explain Goethe and Nietzsche to me, to himself: we couldn't even pronounce their names. The *furor* of the
self-educated man who managed on a few bob a week and hardly
ever mentioned the nights in the shell-holes. 'I was lucky, Sam.
I never got a scratch. I was one of the lucky ones.'

I must mention the drink problem. I can't hide it away. We were
both ready-made alcoholics. What saved us? Lack of opportunity. No money. You see he'd naturally got a taste for the
stuff, what you got to say about it, eh? Goo on, what you gotta
say about it? Ow'd yo a bin if yo'd bin in the bleedin' trenches at
nineteen? Calm down, nobody's got anything to say about it.
What more natural? Poor darling lad, he got a taste for the stuff.
It was really a terribly minor problem, please *dewn't* misunder-
stend mc, stuff me silly, bai *new* means, *naiow* means at all. Just
a slight recurring weakness. Goo for wiks, months even, without

a smell of the stuff. Right Band of Hope blue ribander, wiks on end, quoite eppy with a cup of tea, cupper cocoa, then bosho, bing, bang wham silly buggers, 'e's at it agen. Arf a pint of mild and 'e's off.

Me too. Half a pint of mild and he's off. Weak in the head, what a silly phrase for the chemistry that makes some impervious, or very nearly, some prone, highly pervious. Horace liked a drop of beer and when I found out what a drop of beer was like I liked it too. Echerly it was late on in life when we got to the beer, before that we did our drinking with the aid of several lovely old darls who made homemade wine. Fat old faggots some of them, funny how we had a lot of fat old faggots around while half the population was half starving. All them carbohydrates, I reckon, don't you? Never heard of them till I was past caring, of course, but that's what it would be. You don't have to know the name of the poison, after all.

We got to going round and dropping in. Lovely drop of stuff, that, lad. Some brewed parsnip, mangold, potato; some were specialists in elderberry. But elderberry was not so common, there were a lot of roach fishers round and elderberry trees got stripped sharpish. This was before we ever heard of hempseed as a roach bait. Echerly we used worms, stewed wheat, bread paste, crust, wasp grup from the comb, and home-reared maggots, as a general thing. But in the elderberry season you kept a sharp lookout for elderberries, which were said to be irresistible to roach. I was a bit torn, natch, wanting to rob the tree for my bait and wanting to drink the wine next year. It was life, always like that.

No, mainly parsnip, mangold, and a certain amount of potato, but the two first-named prime and easy favourites. The ladies who made wine, comfortable women all, all the wives of miners, they made us welcome. Horace was welcome in all these homes, all that sort of home. He wasn't unwelcome *anywhere*, but the welcome varied, he was so sweet and easy no one minded him, but them as was getting on in the world a bit, well, you know how they were, kind of *leery* would you say? nervous, edgy, always looking over their shoulders, worrying about picking something up from somebody, like it was infectious. Fag ash on the carpet, too. The poor took it all in their stride, you can't fall off the floor can you? but them as was just edging up a bit, heaving thesselves up by they own bootlaces, that's the sort reckon they might catch something from somebody, don't want to be reminded, ah, if you ask me, who's asking you? all right then, no, but I mean, it was the contagion they were nervous of, they thought a somebody like that with no idea which side his bread was buttered, he might put ideas into their heads, remind them what they were missing, no respect for property, laughing and swigging that home-made wine, fag ash on the rag rug, hobnails scratting the lino, you want to watch it, one false step and you're back in the gutter.

Funny how it went, like calling to like as like as not, there we were slipping craftily across the waste, quiet down back alleys, nipping into colliers' homes where the wine was kept. . . . Roaring old coal fire, free coal of course, in the blackleaded grate; red chenille tablecloth or American cloth or even just newspaper spread on the table, always the same scrubbed deal square table, scrubbed so the harder grain stood proud, horsehair one-ended sofa, granfeyther chur and the rest just churs, kitchen chairs, and a rag rug on the red-tiled hearth, so bonny. Hello, Horace, hello, Sam, come in lads, sit you down, mek room our Florrie, how'd you like a drop of home-made wine? We're away.

Getting back home, across the waste, up the quiet alleys and down the mean streets and into the posh road, the lamp posts irresistible, got to climb just one, anyway. Now watch it, Sam, oh my taters, I slipped, oh God it hurts, I'm ruptured mate, oh my privates. I told you, didn't I? He won't be told.

Funny how the news sometimes got home before we did. Not a soul to be seen in the dark winter evening, but the news gets home. Sadly shaken heads, pursed lips, lad, lad, how many times do I have to tell you? You ought to know better. Always the cold douche of respectability. Constraint over supper, the evening ruined all round, everybody unhappy. Mutterings. At his age, too. Leading him on. *I* don't know what'll become of him, I tell you, I really don't. Next day, quiet, a suffocating sort of silence. Next day after that, all forgotten, well, not precisely *forgotten*, but say no more about it, let's pretend it never happened. But it did happen. It happened too often to be an accident. No smoke without fire.

How many evenings, sitting on hard kitchen chairs set round the walls of little living rooms, kitchens, with red fires, oil lamps,

sometimes gas mantles, never electricity; the dad in his chair by
the fire, the mom sitting with an elbow on the table, hand to
forehead or chin, the immemorial stoic stance, her little interval
of rest in a hard day; the growing-up ones drinking it all in, the
mugs and tumblers of home-made wine going down, the talk and
the singing.... Poor people's good cheer, economic, only cost
the price of a few pounds of parsnips, a few mangolds snitched
from farmer's field in the dusk of a winter day, a few pounds of
sugar, a screw of yeast from the brewery.... Good cheer, good
companions, heady wine, a price to pay in respectability, who
cared?

Marked men, in a small way. Not quite reliable in some curious
other sense. Mark you, reliable as Sunday morning in the
ordinary sense: what we said we'd do for you, we did. Paint
your house for you, we did that, get the load of coal in from the
street if the man was laid up, run errands, chop a bit of kindling,
'sit with' somebody who was a 'a bit down', sick visiting, form-
filling, write you a letter as soon as look at you, mediate in rows,
wash up, get down and scrub a floor, oh yes, anything like that,
quite dependable. But in that other funny way, y'know, *funny*....
Neither of us seemed quite to know which side his bread was
buttered, or even to care. All that funny talk about Jesus,
Shelley, Blake, Dostoievsky.... Yards of poetry, always singing
out loud going along the road, playing the fool, look more like
tramps than – no, that's not fair, that's going too far, they'm not
that bad, only, funny – ay it? – they don't seem to mind how they
look or what anybody thinks on 'em. I tell you very confidentially,
they didn't.

All this time I was drifting towards being a member of the
bourgeois establishment, provincial sector, grade three. It's the
same right through, that cake, from Whitehall and Buckingham
Pal right down through the county people and the Kensington
people and every other sort of people who take the hierarchical
social structure and their own place in it seriously. What Horace
taught me first, I mean he was the first to open my eyes to it,
was that the open society is the only society worth living for,
never mind dying for. Not free exactly, freedom is illusion, but
classless, open; free at any rate of caste. I was drifting towards
another caste, even I could see it, Horace could see it, nothing
anyone could do, not even me with my idleness and derision,

could stop the process from working itself out, to a certain extent, superficially anyway, simply because I was bright enough to pass the exams standing on my thin skull; and I had certain special talents, how absurd to deny it. But I'll say this, all the time I drifted 'up' like a slightly leaky gas-filled bladder, I never lost touch; I might have been rising, but nobody else was falling on that account, I wasn't climbing up on somebody else's neck. Once a mate, always a mate.

Mates. What am I talking about? When I had become a Grade A fully paid-up member of the professional establishment I met some of the loveliest fellows you ever set eyes on, some of the best friends, best company, cracking good chaps, brave and true, entertaining and stimulating. And some right shite-hawks, too. But you find that sort in any grade.

Mates. I'm sentimentalising again. No, not altogether. Fallible memory is not wholly at sea. The best compost for friendship is that earthy loam, free from the acids of envy, in which the strangling shoots of ambition can't get a hold.

I went to Horace's funeral. Several of his mates from the factory turned up. What they had to say about him was what I expected to hear. This was years after the end of our intimacy, you understand. Years. Not of estrangement, but of absence: growing away. The way they spoke of him, that was the epitaph a man earns only by being the right stuff all through. You can't counterfeit it. A man who simply doesn't know the meaning of treachery or (in his own personal sense) exploitation. Of course he *did* know the meaning of exploitation – he was exploited all his life, his life was a reaction against all exploitation. To him, another human being was just a human being, one of us, not 'one of our sort'. Silly, sensitive, dear old fool, he really did *believe* in human dignity, in the free soul, in *the holiness of the heart's affections* (Keats). I don't mean he never had an enemy or never disliked anybody, of course he did, but he never tried to put anybody down. He was always trying to lift people up. He had a pure innate delicacy of feeling about human relations, the exquisite tact of the natural gentleman.

I hope I haven't given the impression that he was always serious. He was serious, all right, he was one of the most serious men I ever knew; but he was also one of the gayest. When he was younger he was wonderfully light-hearted. He praised his

God like the medieval tumblers and jongleurs, by laughter and jests and song, by dancing and playing the fool. In the worst of the hard times, before a little relative affluence (by God, it was relative) softened his circumstances just that little bit, in those hard times he was as transparent as a crystal jug, the light of sheer goodness and gaiety shone right through him. He'd give you his last ha'penny but he'd give it with a joke. He was full of pity and absolutely empty of self-pity. He had less self-pity than anyone I've known. Later he grew quieter, of course; the burden of staying gay is a lot to bear. He even grew a little stubborn, pig-headed: but still only in a negative sense, rejecting well-meant advice, not pig-headed in furthering his own ends.

He used to smoke a lot. We both did. His favourite tobacco was called Sweet Memories. But we also smoked Erinmore, as I still do, and at Christmas only we lashed out on an ounce of Gold Block, when it cost over a shilling, well over a shilling, monstrous. Normally our tobacco cost sevenpence or eightpence an ounce. We used to take the dog Jack for walks, a rough-haired Irish terrier with a heart as silly as our own. If we had the means, we'd nip in to a pub near the canal for half a pint of mild. Sometimes we all three had to share it. The dogs always loved him. He was gentle, you know, a gentleman.

And a loser.

Though not in my book.

6

Teachers

MR HEADMASTER was headmaster of the junior school when I arrived there, clutching my scholarship, shortly before my eleventh birthday. I'm afraid we each made a rather bad impression on the other. I could tell right away that I was not the kind of little boy Mr Headmaster liked best. He reserved his approbation, of which quality he had only a limited quantity, for compact little boys in neat navy-blue serge or grey flannel suits, with slicked-down hair, gleaming teeth, square little shoulders and square little heads. He did not need to tell me that I was a disappointment to him. Nevertheless he told me. He was not pleased by my posture, which was negligent, my clothes, which were not quite right, my head, which was narrow with a low forehead and distended back, my hair, which was wavy, my teeth, which were rather poor having been cruelly messed about with by a sadistic old bastard who practised as a dentist though he would have been more at home in a concentration camp, yanking out the gold fillings.

My posture was negligent not because I wished it to be – how fervently I wished it otherwise – but because I was naturally spindly and frail, was gaining height fast, had chronic digestive and bowel trouble and ate unsuitable food at irregular intervals. This was many years before the system of school dinners was instituted. I either carried sandwiches or was given a small sum of dinner money which naturally I spent on almost anything except nourishing food. For one reason and another, I was not an athletic type. My small store of physical energy was usually exhausted by the time I had completed the three-mile journey to school. No one seemed aware of this, and I was unwilling to admit it even to myself. I threw myself into every boyish activity, trusting that a considerable store of nervous energy would mask the physical deficiencies. By the time I had dragged myself home, usually with stomach-ache, I was so drained that homework became a nightmare. I was well into my teens before some sort of balance was restored and my stomach upsets became less frequent.

But if I was not Mr Headmaster's ideal type of little boy, he was far from being my ideal type of man. He was the first dandy I had met. He wore double-breasted waistcoats to his elegant suits, usually of pin-striped blue flannel; his hair was carefully waved; he wore rings and a tie-pin and the handkerchief in his breast pocket was arranged beautifully. To crown the lot he wore spats: pearl grey. His flesh was pale and pudgy, his eyes small and, at any rate when he looked in my direction, unfriendly.

Mr Headmaster's disapprobation reached its peak one ghastly morning when I carried a letter to school from my father. It was undoubtedly a letter which should never have been delivered; like so many. Angry letters are a therapeutic thing to write, but are usually best not posted. Since I was the postman in this case, I caught the full brunt of the effect. It was my first experience of the power of the written word.

One dreary winter afternoon I had been engaging Stan Crow in conversation when we should both have been doing something else, such as algebra. A very nice assistant master named, if I remember rightly, Mr Ashley, regretfully but firmly told us both to write out twice an immensely long and maudlin Anglican hymn. Stan Crowe dutifully wrote his two fair copies, but when I told my father – who asked what I was doing – about this imposition, he flew into a splendid rage and dashed off a wonderfully eloquent letter to poor Mr A. As a staunch nonconformist he was sickened not only by the high-handedness of the imposition, which impinged on civil liberties, but by the theological enormity of the task. 'All human conflict is ultimately theological,' Cardinal Newman once said to the young Hilaire Belloc; and I'm sure that my father's objection was not so much to the fact of punishment, as to the nature of it. It was the hymn he objected to as much as the sheer uselessness of the chore.

When father was roused he could be wonderfully abusive in a sort of abstract way. He did not know the man he was rebuking; there was nothing personal in it; he was simply enjoying himself as a theoretical libertarian assailing the citadels of established privilege and autocracy. It was a very fine intemperate tract which he penned, a real Black Country diatribe from the heart of one of our most rhetorical local preachers. By the time he had written a rough draft, read it aloud two or three times to try out its flavour on us, and finally made a fair copy incorporating several afterthoughts of cutting wit, the whole family had wasted more time than it would have taken me to copy out my hymn twice. And we'd *all* been involved: my sisters' homework, too, was irremediably dislocated. But it made a most enjoyable diversion. This was a long time before television came in.

Poor dear Mr Ashley, who was really a very gentle person and had been tried beyond endurance, I don't doubt, took it very badly. I think he was freshly down from Oxford with a poor degree; how else would he have landed up teaching the first year at the junior school? 'I'm one who doesn't like getting a letter like this,' he said to me miserably. I understood instantly, and my whole state of mind changed like an egg flipped over in a pan. What he was confiding in me was that he too was a diffident and rather shy person, not a fighter who would welcome a letter like that as a challenge to a thoroughly enjoyable barney. I was on his side immediately, and not for the first nor the last time in my life experienced the pangs of 'seeing both sides' of a dispute. I was still proud of dad's polemic, but wished it had not been inflicted on Mr Ashley, who from that moment was gathered into the fold of my charity as a sufferer like other sufferers. But it was too late. 'I shall have to show it to Mr Headmaster,' he said sadly. 'I'm afraid your father really leaves me no alternative.'

Mr Headmaster took it very badly, too. He wrote to my father and requested his attendance. This was a fearful nuisance; dad was very busy in his building business, which was rocky, and anyway he had forgotten the letter as soon as it was despatched. But he made the time, and he and Mr Headmaster were closeted together in the Head's study for a long time. Dad left without seeing me, and at home that evening I realised that he had been worsted in the argument. Perhaps he, too, had never before met a man quite like Mr Headmaster, who was arrogant, lofty in manner, condescending, and no fool. I gathered that dad shared my distaste for the tyrant, but have no doubt that the tyrant made it quite clear that he was going to run the school his way and if father didn't like it he could take me away. Of course father had no such intention.

I think Mr Headmaster scored the most telling point when he put it to father that as a businessman and employer of a labour force he must know the absolute basic necessity of discipline. At any rate, from that moment on the old radical looked the other way. I was left – very properly, I thought: I was really very much relieved – to be beaten, slippered, cuffed, caned and awarded such condign punishments as detention and endless impositions, as and when my conduct called for correction. I never questioned the justice that was meted out. It should always be possible, for an intelligent person, to imagine the commission of any crime. Not to be able to do so implies a defective imagination. But if one can imagine the crime, one must also accept the punishment. This I have always found it easy to do. To repudiate it, I mean imaginatively, is to repudiate the concept of 'justice, the contribution of our star'. Justice is so absolutely a unique human concept that I cannot bring myself to do this. One's whole life must be a debate between justice and liberty, and in the end justice may prevail. *Fiat justicia ruat coelum.*

Mr Headmaster was the first autocrat from another world (i.e., not from our village) to impose his notion of justice upon me and to restrict my liberty. In a sense he was the first establishment figure in my life, for while the village teachers at the elementary schools exercised great authority, it was done in concert with one's family, they were visible known neighbours, figures in the same mythology, cut from the same cloth as ourselves. There was nothing abstract in their justice: the whole village, families interlinked, connived in it.

Mr Headmaster's justice was Olympian. He gave me bad reports, which were richly deserved, and I have, I hope, repaid him in kind. Is it really important to impress on little boys of ten notions of their inadequacy? Have we not suffered enough for two thousand years from the persistent humiliation of the human spirit imposed by superstition? The psyche is mutilated by religion and deformed by authoritarianism. No, perhaps it is not brilliant to make little boys of ten feel socially inferior, mentally retarded; to make them aware of vast gulfs between their puny weakling selves and the coruscating aristocracy of their confident elders. Was father right or wrong to knuckle down and leave me to learn the system of carrot-and-stick? I'm not sure. Though I was relieved to be left to learn it, though the innate touch of masochism and the natural awe of excellence made me anxious to be left alone to suffer, to learn the despair of the stiff upper lip, though I do not reproach him but love his memory the more, yet I suspect now that his passionate outburst of libertarian eloquence was right and his subsequent conversion to the spurious philosophy of the stiff upper lip was wrong. O the reticent English, how much they miss by biting back those words of joy and grief.

By the time I was transferred to the main school, after a first year at the junior, I was already versed in the ways of dissimulation and a practised tyrant-spotter. I bear no grudge, I harbour no malice, against the team of educators who saw me through from guileless affectionate boy to guileful affectionate young man. Some of them were plainly marking time, watching the clock, in it for the money. Not that the money was anything special, but in those times it was something to have security, a regular income and the status of dominie. But there were several who were in it from conviction, born pedagogues with passions and prejudices about the art of education.

The new wave of liberal education had not yet begun to flow, we were living through the last years of the authoritarian pipe-dream. The Great War had in fact fatally wrecked the old authoritarianism, man had seen through it, but this knowledge was still locked away, hidden in innumerable brave and aching hearts. It took several decades for it to filter down through the strata of social imperatives, to percolate the rocky shale of social habits and that almost impermeable reluctance to admit new ideas. We still had Hitlerism and fascism ahead of us, not to mention the horrors of Stalinism and Maoism. We are still not really through it and out into the virgin pastures of the open society. We have a final struggle yet to wage, against the inborn reactionary terror, the nostalgic yearning that springs from fear. But the way to the open society is now clearly signposted and it will be ridiculous if we lose our way. But at the time of which I write, a few years after Armageddon, men were still unwilling to admit what they knew in their hearts to be true, that the authoritarian system was a dead loss, a failure, an insult to the human potentiality, a slur on the innate dignity of man.

Incredibly, inertia overcame the awakening; the weakness for known order was strangely stronger than the urge to accept one another as brothers. Through the terrible years of the 'Twenties we allowed the old bombinating humbugs to re-assert their hold on us. We could not bring ourselves to admit that the 'dear brave lads' who had given their lives in the war had been had for suckers. We knew it, deep down, but we could not quite admit it, it seemed somehow a slur on their courage and their sacrifice. So we rebuilt the structure of authoritarian humbug, shakily it is true, and went on pretending that *dulce et decorum est, pro patria mori*. We could not yet admit that our *patria* was a shoddy market place run by delusion and greed and conniving. We still had a war ahead of us, just one more war.

The masters represented the spectrum of illusion and self-deception very fairly. There were dear dim old boys who still really believed in playing the game and keeping a straight bat, and there were one or two at the opposite end of the spectrum who had an inkling of another truth. These views were not polarised, there was a nominal unanimity, but in personal terms tthe poles were neatly represented by on my right, in the true-blue corner, representing cricket and the military virtues, Crop Thomas, and on my left, representing Marxism and atheism, A. E. Clarke.

These were the outstanding characters though there were several sturdy teachers who were characterful enough in the ordinary sense, being self-sufficient, dependable, limited square-heads unlikely to lead a lad into fresh pastures of thought but on the other hand equally unlikely to lead him into fresh pastures of villainy. But Crop and A. E. were cut from different cloth. Crop was a crew-cut Welshman, tall and saturnine, who had won the Military Cross in the said war and who lived for cricket, poetry, and the school. A. E. was a slightly baggy, pale, intense historian, freshly down from St John's College, Cambridge, who wore a red tie and ostentatiously failed to take part in the hymns which we sang at assembly. He lolled against the oak panelling, wearing a sneer, and with his hands conspicuously in his pockets, when we sang *Floreat Regina, schola Mariae* and *Forty Years On* and *God Save Our Gracious King*. I have heard that in later years A. E. moderated his opinions, even joined the Anglican church, and ended up a pillar of society. What more natural? But at this time he was our living revolutionary and as such the most interesting master in the school, bar none. We did not necessarily love or even admire him for it, but we harkened.

I felt some awe for them both, though my real affection was reserved for other masters, now hazy in my memory, on whom I had the usual boyish crushes. I find it strange and sad that I cannot now recall much of the young masters to whom I gave my affection; I should not know them if I saw them again. But Crop and A. E. have lived with me throughout the more-than-forty years which have elapsed since I left their tutelage. Crop taught me, not so much history of which he dispensed a version that even at the time I felt to be eccentric, but to respect the poet and the soldier, language and courage. I know now that courage is not enough – it is useless without intelligence and affection. I know now that language is not enough – it is useless without affection and a strong visual and tactile sense. In certain circumstances both qualities, courage and articulacy, are worse than useless, they make things worse. But you have to know them before you can choose the right moment to discard them, and my debt to Crop is considerable.

In addition, he gave the dangerous bonus of personality. He was without doubt the most considerable personality in the school: he had in abundance what we now call charisma. Though keen enough on cricket and the corporate ethos of the school, he also dispensed a sort of sardonic rasping humour which suggested to us that he was not taken in by shibboleths. Beneath that close-cropped hair and above that brindled moustache, his dark eyes flashed in his dark Celtic face, flashed with ire and also with a humour that was nothing if not sardonic; sometimes savage. God knows what he thought of A. E.

A. E. was struggling against something, of that one was aware even as a boy. He was not well-endowed superficially. He was pale and puffy, he had no idea how to wear clothes, his handwriting was atrocious, his voice was not melodious. But all this was as nothing alongside the fury of his mental drive. He drove us to learn and to think. History as he taught it was a frontal assault on the shibboleth system. While Crop taught dates and battles, A. E. taught social history, history as a record of exploitation and intrigue, corruption and economic necessity. He opened our eyes to the fact that, as Lenin put it, history is the story of *who, whom?* I learned later, from the French communist Thorez, that 'history is the propaganda of the victors' (and later still discerned that it is becoming the propaganda of the vanquished). This was the definitive liberation. True, it was to be lost again, overlaid by a period of intoxication when I fell under the malign spell of Chesterton, Belloc and a rather lazy-minded Oxford tutor – a time when rhetoric won a temporary but damaging victory over reason. But A. E. had sown the seed. Having once absorbed the truth that history is the story of man's exploitation of everything exploitable, I was never henceforward susceptible to the flattery of success. Though he had no intention of doing anything of the kind, A. E. by making me suspicious of success made me unduly fond of failure.

Needless to say, A. E. himself never saw to the heart of that paradox. He wanted his boys to get on. He urged us to work harder. He was pleased when we won scholarships and exhibitions. Though he despised the trappings of ostentatious self-indulgence – 'When I was at St John's I lunched on bread and cheese every day' – though ascetic and intellectually severe, he took a natural pride in the achievements of his students and did not invariably notice that some of them were already exploiting him and everyone in sight. I was myself a late developer, and he held out no great hope of success for one so idle and sceptical. But when I won my modest successes – the Shute Open Exhibition and a School Leaving Exhibition – he mellowed towards me and showed an affectionate side to his austere nature which he had not shown before. He was rightly sceptical of my tutor's confident prediction, based on a precocious essay style which I cannot now reproduce, that I should get a First, and regarded my Third as confirmation of his superior insight into my character rather than as a reflection on his teaching ability. In doing so he was entirely justified.

It was A. E. who accurately predicted my success in popular journalism. I had written an intemperate essay on one of the less attractive characteristics of the Augustan Age, and when he publicly rebuked me for the vehemence of my language, remarking quite properly that such vehemence would militate against academic success, I hotly disavowed any wish for academic success and asserted that I intended to become a journalist. If I had said I intended to become a pimp he could hardly have been more shocked. Yes, he supposed, shaking his head sadly, the Press was probably the best avenue for me to explore. The Yellow Press, for preference. It went down very well with the layabouts of the Modern Sixth, of course. To do A. E. justice – and I wish to do him no less – he sturdily refused to be pleased by my quite reasonable, indeed quite spectacular success on the Yellow Press, but he mellowed towards me when I became a respectable critic on the respectable *Sunday Times*.

He married a most attractive young woman, who used to entertain his Sixth Form boys to tea from time to time. I think several of us enjoyed fantasies of intimacy with her. I know I did. Fantasies of concupiscence were rife among the boys of the Modern Sixth, at any rate among the boys who were my familiars. No reasonably comely female was safe from our imaginative prurience. Though all were entirely safe in the real, physical sense. We had the hots for everything in silk stockings, but behaved ourselves like the young gentlemen we were being trained to emulate. I don't know if A. E. knew what a nest of dreamers he presided over. His vision of history was almost exclusively economic; sex did not come into it. Incomplete!

I cannot remember that A. E. ever punished anyone. He didn't need to. His wrath was hard to bear; his disdain of idleness and sloppy thinking were punishment enough. He treated us like men, albeit unfinished men; his lessons were all tutorials in the Cambridge sense. He taught us how to gut a book, taking furious and copious notes. He despised the dilettante approach and revered scholarship, though he was not a vainglorious pot hunter, either personally or vicariously. If he had a shortcoming as a teacher, it was that he lacked a little the warmth, the genial flash of paradox, that illuminates learning in the approach of the very finest teachers. A. E. never relaxed. His style was a little too austere for us weaker brethren, who needed to be beguiled into learning. But he illuminated history with a cold white light. I should have benefited more from his teaching had I met him a little later, as an undergraduate. I think he was a *don manqué*. I needed such a don.

Four teachers remain in my memory as figures of affection. Crop Thomas and A. E. Clarke at grammar school; Mr Fryer and Mr Hadderley – or was it Mr Adderley? – at elementary school. Mr Fryer had a bullet through his leg on the Somme; Mr Hadderley – or Mr Adderley – lost an eye in Flanders. When I knew them they seemed middle-aged, though now I know that they were quite youngish men, freshly returned from the battle-fields. They exuded a sort of inner quiet. It might not be going too far to suggest that they were struck dumb by the shock of war. They were certainly very quiet, reserved men, gentle to the very limits of tolerance, deeply reluctant to raise their voices in reproach or to administer punishment. I was very fond of them at the time and later I came to realise that in a sense they were sleep-walking through what remained of life, they were listening, in a sort of incredulity, to the silence that had fallen after the battle. They might have disowned any such interpretation but that would not necessarily make it invalid.

Over the whole plateau, windy, cold, ugly, stricken, there seemed to brood a quietness, a great deep quietness of shock and outrage; numb. We were too young to quite understand, but some attenuated fraction of the truth must have sidled in under our tender skins, for there was a reserve even in our rumbustiousness, we did not push insolence to its natural limits. Bereavement brooded over the village like a cold cloud. Survivors tempered in war knew themselves betrayed but kept the knowledge to themselves. Women wrecked by loss found it hard to smile but they kept quiet too. Everyone seemed aware that the basis of life had been found flawed, and fatally. But everyone kept quiet about it. It was as if no one wanted to be the first to admit that it had become unbearable. Quiet stoic people, too long-suffering, too meek, too brave. It would be easy to say, too gullible. But I don't believe they were gullible; I believe they *knew*, and they had rumbled to it, they had seen the chasm opening up and glimpsed the hideous interior of the bottomless pit. But being brought up to suffer and endure without a whimper, soldiered on quietly. I wonder now if this was wrong. Perhaps we should have risen with a cry of grief and rage and brought the pillars of the temple crashing down, and from the rubble of illusion and deceit joyfully built our new Jerusalem. But that was not what we were taught to do: and besides, we did not know how to do it. There was no blueprint for the new Jerusalem. There still isn't. And we had been taught to soldier on, quietly; and if possible, to 'better ourselves'.

Three of my four favourite teachers, ex-soldiers all, abetted this proposition (though to be sure it was all tacit, never explicit). The fourth, just too young to have been a soldier, showed a way through the rubble. I am grateful to them all for their witness and example, both false and true. They helped to make me the creature I became, so various and multiplex.

It is not their fault, it is my own, if I have lived six decades with the hope that things may not be what they seem. If, now, at long last, I begin to suspect that original sin may indeed be a fundamental fact of human life, I can only blame myself for having been so slow in the uptake. If, now, I begin to suspect that far from the soul being mutilated by religion and deformed by authority, it is in desperate need of those disciplines for its healthy growth ... if now I see order and self-discipline as the imperatives for a healthy and just society, a good life.... Well, I must be an even later developer than I thought.

But I did not wish to cook the book.

7

Eddie

RUNNING down the long reverse slope of the railway bridge in Broad Lane I took a real fistful, twisted the old twist-grip as far round as it would come and set the Coventry Eagle singing. It was a modest song at the best of times but you can only do the best with what you've got. I suppose we might have touched 50. The idea was, always, to wind it up down this long slope of the railway bridge and take the humpbacked canal bridge, which followed immediately, flat-out. If you actually took off, if you were aware of thin air underneath you before you touched down on the other side, you felt rather good.

I felt quite good. I knew we were airborne, me and the old Eagle. She was only a pedestrian 172 c.c. Villiers, the older engine with the non-detachable cylinder head and the cast-iron piston. You couldn't tune her. But she had twin exhaust pipes, grandly plated in the new-fangled chrome. She looked like 55 even when she was only the old honest 45. Some people were strangers to the truth but I knew we were generally speaking a full 10 m.p.h. short of the new Villiers, and *that* was only good for a useful 55 at the best of times.

As we touched down on the far side of the canal bridge something exploded in my right or offside lug, a great rousing crash of moving air displaced by moving machinery. Eddie Dawson on his KSS Velocette shot past and began to draw away down the long lovely straight that led to Essington. There was never a hope in hell, of course; he could beat us in second gear or alternatively with snow shoes on. But I got down to it, with my behind on the rear mudguard and my chin on the tank and the slide practically pulled out of the carburettor.

Eddie dwindled in the distance, of course, but after a time he must have backed off and the distance began to decrease. He waited at the end of the straight, where the road forked, and eventually we hauled up alongside.

'Where did you get your pipes chromed?' Eddie asked. So I told him.

And that was my first conversational exchange with the boy who was to become, in fullness of time, my oldest surviving friend. I'm going back a good forty-two years now. We were both seventeen, one of the greatest ages there is. Or are. I had seen Eddie around for several years, and wished to get to know him, but we were both shy lads, though heaven knows he was shyer than I was. He was one of the shyest lads in the town, which was Walsall, Staffs.

It was rather odd that he should be so shy, since he was a butcher with a shop of his own, serving the Walsall populace with their necessities in the protein line, day in, day out. However, there it is: he was a very shy lad. I suppose the fact is that in a shop there is a certain formality and limitation of exchanges, a convention of sociableness – and furthermore, there is a ready-made, cast-iron excuse for speaking to strangers, on both sides of the counter. Shopping, I've sometimes thought, is for many people a substitute for social intercourse, it *is* their social intercourse. Safely limited, needing no excuses, unlikely to take you into deeper water than you wish to tread.

A shop of his own at seventeen? Yes. That's the sort of lad he was: wholly dependable, grown-up, diligent, sober, sensible. The only thing Eddie was mad about was motorbikes. And Irene. And perhaps fishing. In everything else, at seventeen he was as dependable, as reliable, as mature as most middle-aged men. But vastly more adventurous. Don't think he was dull: on the contrary.

Eddie's family, the Dawsons, owned two butchers' shops in the town. Dad ran the original home shop, over which the family lived. The second was opened for Eddie, or taken over for Eddie, can't remember now, just a couple of hundred yards away along Stafford Street. It's still there, and so is my old friend. He's been there forty-three years, since he was sixteen.

'My life doesn't change much, Sam,' he said to me the other day. And I thought how true, how remarkable, how absolutely splendid. When I feel sick and unsteady, a bit low, sickened by the news or racked by the cheapness and racketty vulgarity of London and Home Counties' life, the go-getters' rat race, I think of Eddie and the splendid stability of his character and his life, and I'm reassured.

He was an old young man and now he is a young old man. It follows. It isn't paradox. The stability, the straight-line direct- ness and truth of his nature, were always there, born in, built in. He is calm and serene because he has nothing to regret. He has ploughed his furrow die-straight from headland to headland. Well, thank God, he hasn't reached the ultimate far headland yet, but he's getting on, and he can look back or look forward and see the die-straight line, the perfect sober craftsmanship of his passage through life, undeviating and admirable.

But we've got away from his straight-line undeviating passage down Broad Lane on the Velocette. We had passed one another before this, I on my tiddly little two-strokes, first the Alldays Allon which cost £6 and then the Coventry Eagle (what an ironical name) which cost £20; Eddie on his much more costly and fascinating bikes, first a 350 New Imperial, then a beautiful 350 Model 8 Sunbeam, and now the Velo. Shyness kept us from speaking, but now Eddie had hit upon this exemplary impersonal opening gambit, 'Where did you get your pipes chromed?' Life- long friendships have doubtless opened on less dramatic opening gambits, but not much.

I think my answer impressed Eddie. I was able to tell him that the glamorous, glittering exhaust pipes had been chromium- plated at our family works. Nickel plating ruled until 1929; it was nice, indeed nicer than chrome, softer in colour. But it had to be cleaned with metal polish every few days, or after every shower. It was very vulnerable to neglect. And it wore off. The big thing about chromium plating was its imperviousness. You could leave it out all night in the rain and it wouldn't go as nickel went. And some actually liked its cold hard glitter. Anyway, it was just coming in, so it was all the rage. Eddie's bike was worth five times as much as mine and was ten times more potent and desirable, but, being 1929, it had only nickel plate. So you see, Eddie had chosen precisely the opening gambit that worked among the young.

Actually my cousin Wilfred personally plated my pipes for me, as a cousinly gesture. Wilfred was Works Director of J. & J. Wiggin Ltd, Old Hall Works, Revival Street, Bloxwich, and he introduced chromium plating to the factory, and as I say he condescended to give mine the treatment personally, duffing them up on the buffing machines while I watched, entranced. He made a lovely job of them, too. I sold the wretched bike later solely on the strength of those chromium-plated twin exhaust pipes, which were its best feature, and by a considerable margin.

The ice being broken, Eddie and I got down to a pessimistic technical analysis of the Coventry Eagle, which was on the point of seizing up after its blind along Broad Lane. Not for the first time. Its performance was truly pitiful, totally belying its looks. Something symbolical there? Shouldn't wonder. Anyway, its wretched performance did me a good turn, for it rapidly became obvious that two machines so preposterously ill-matched as the Eagle and the Velocette could not travel together in any comfort, so what was the obvious solution? We both rode Eddie's.

So began my actual acquaintance with *fast* motor cycles. Eddie was generosity itself and often let me take over, though he was a far better natural rider, at any rate in the road racing sense. (I was good on the rough stuff, a good trials man.) His reflexes were superb, his judgment very good, though, as time was to prove, not entirely infallible. He was also very strong, a sturdy, indeed burly boy, thick and muscular and trained by his trade to muscular exertion which was quite beyond me. On the pillion behind him I felt safer than behind any other rider.

Though we are still friends after all these years, our really close friendship only spanned a few years, through from boyhood to manhood. Our paths diverged, I went first to Birmingham and then to London. Eddie stayed where he was. But in those half-dozen halcyon years from seventeen on, our relationship was peculiarly rich and good.

It was, in a sense, the friendship of opposites. I don't say David and Jonathan precisely, but the very fact that we were unalike in so many respects, but still shared certain vital interests and ideals, welded our friendship solidly, tenaciously, against all strains. We were almost laughably complementary. Eddie was stocky, strong, quiet, reserved, highly practical. I was none of those things, to put it shortly. Eddie did not stay on at school; I began to think I'd never leave school. Eddie read quite a bit but loathed writing letters; I enjoyed writing letters more than most occupations. Eddie was rich, by my standards; I was poor by his. Eddie was brave in a quiet, lasting, apparently effortless way – he was brave right through, it never occurred to him to be anything else. I had to screw my courage up nervously to take the risks we took. Or any risks. Eddie was (and is) the most consistent, all-of-one-piece person you could wish to meet. My middle name is change.

Yet we got on marvellously. I hero-worshipped Eddie from the start; he had so many of the qualities I admired and felt myself to lack. I think Eddie quite admired some of my more flashy and meretricious qualities. At least I amused him, I think. Which is more than I'm doing now for you, reader me old dear, isn't it? Yes, I know. Somehow you seem to lose the knack. I'd love to; I'd love to amuse *me*.

Eddie never let me work in his shop, in the sense of cutting up meat and dishing it out to the customers, but he let me lean on the counter for as long as I liked, and, in fact, when the counter had had enough of that and began to sag under the strain, Eddie let me help him build a new and massive counter, shelves, and so on, even if my role amounted to little more than holding tools, handing up the screws, pressing from the other side against the screwdriver, supporting timbers on my back, and so on; all the unskilled labourer's chores. I liked that.

I liked watching him cut up, too. It was a poor district and he sold a lot of frozen imported meat, and the way the knife used to *hiss* through the grainy, almost bloodless textures fascinated me. He was a craftsman, of course. The anti-surgery of the butcher, dismembering the carcass which has already lost its identity with the living animal, reducing it steadily to *helpings* which finally cease to bear any relationship with the beast that walked – chops, steaks, fillets, joints – there's a very strange engrossment in watching this process. I watched it for hours on end, time after time, learning the different colours of the days and the components of the days.... Light on Tuesdays, light on Wednesdays, warming up Thursdays, ruddy Fridays. I never intruded on Saturday, the day when Eddie made about eighty per cent of his week's sale; he closed on Monday, knowing there would be nobody to buy, and as often as not we went fishing, or chasing over the March of Wales or up the spine of Staffordshire to the Cheshire meres.

The Velocette was followed by a Sunbeam Model 9, 'the greatest', and the Sunbeam by a Super Sports Morgan, and the Morgan by a J2 M.G. Midget.... Those four vehicles – if we dare call them vehicles when they were so clearly magic carpets, transformation devices, cowboys' horses, instruments of liberty and illusion – those four spell out and encompass and delimit the years of maximum euphoria. The changes in my own life could scarcely have been more dramatic; from sixth-form school-boy to Oxford undergraduate to published poet and polemical satirist to working journalist ... meanwhile Eddie's life remained, as he puts it, unchanged. There was an ingredient here, in this friendship of apparent incompatibles, of complementary qualities, which I think is singularly interesting. It was as if we both recog-nised the pull of polarities ... the centripetal pull of Eddie's rooted stability on the one hand; on the other the strange attrac-tion of my obvious centrifugal instability, the whirl of my life which threatened at all times to throw me off the edge of the known world, *our* world, flying off, spinning off into the dark unknowable void of life-styles and experiences neither of us could quite imagine. Eddie did not really want to come with me, and I, though part of me urgently wanted to remain in the known world, did not really want to stay. The contrast gave a flavour to our friendship, a tension of conflicting impulses which heightened the savour. In a real sense, when finally I did fly off, disappear over the horizon, bound for that strange exotic never-never land, Eddie was the home I left behind me. Drifting and spinning through that dark-blue void shot with the incandescent brilliance of comets, nebulae and exploding stars, I often thought of Eddie still standing there behind the counter, sturdy in his white butcher's uniform, sharpening the knife, serving the people, Tuesday, Wednesday, Thursday, Friday and crowded Saturday.

A fixed star. Enviable and reassuring.

Eddie was not only a motorcycle and sports car fan, he was also a good fisherman and a fine shot. Later he became a keen golfer, but that is another experience we never shared. The chief experience which we did share was our joy in the open road, in speed. We had some hair-raising struggles with enthusiasts on Nortons, A.J.S.s, B.S.A.s, Scotts, Panthers, Singer Nines, Amilcars, T.T. Triumphs, and other M.G.s, and we had some awkward moments. 'Coming off' the bike was an ordinary hazard, taken very lightly, though one black day Edwin had his skull fractured by the blunt end of a lorry which turned sharp right on the Perry Bar road just as he was pulling out to overtake, on the KSS Velo. Eddie discharged himself after about forty-eight hours in hospital; with a fractured skull, yes. He discharged himself because his innate modesty and delicacy simply wouldn't permit him to be nursed by girls, to use the bottle and the bed-pan. I never knew a man who had such great delicacy of feeling in that respect. He never told a dirty story, or listened to one.

He married the girl whom he was courting when first we met, at the age of seventeen. (So did I, for that matter.) Eddie's girl, Irene, was then a schoolgirl; in fact he was killing time before he picked her up from Elmore Green School, to run her home on the pillion, when we had our first little race along the Broad Lane testing straight. So it must have been a Monday or a Wednesday. He never had another girl, or thought of one. Eddie and Irene duly married; their first home was a flat over the shop, which Eddie fitted out himself; quite soon they bought a house in Broadway North and they live in it to this day; they had two daughters and now they are grandparents. An undeviating straight line, the perfect linear graph line of development, maturity, contentment. Make of it what you will; to me it is deeply enviable.

You see how Eddie became one of my fixed points of reference. He was, and is, a living proof that *normality* is not a statistical abstraction, but a true possibility. Well, not a proof, maybe, but at any rate evidence, and persuasive evidence. Evidence for the defence. I return to it from time to time when the strain of dubiety grows great. A fastidious scepticism brings its own harvest of bitter fruit, and sometimes, when the palate tingles too much and you feel you must have a sweetener or fall ill, I think of Eddie.

What I have quite failed to bring out in this memoir is the
fun he was. He was grand company. Eddie was a very intelligent
boy who grew into a sagacious man without the benefit of too
too much book learning. His sense of balance was good – I mean
mentally as well as physically. Though rooted in practicality, he
had his full share of appreciation of the bizarre and the romantic.
He enjoyed jokes and sometimes made them – and surprisingly
acute, even sardonic, they could be. But by and large the joy
of his companionship sprang from his simple, innate goodness
of heart, from the absolute conviction that possessed you that he
would never let you down, would face any situation calmly and
with a slight smile. We got ourselves into some pretty tight
corners, from time to time, mainly from our habit of accepting
the challenge of anything on wheels or the challenge of any type
of surface or gradient. Separately and together, we took some
tosses. Eddie was driving one day when I became involved in
one of the more spectacular of the thirteen accidents in which
I have been involved as a passenger.

I was in my last year at Oxford and the day before we had
celebrated, with a certain amount of misgiving which everyone
present strove nobly to conceal, my twenty-first birthday. 1933.
I was 'living out' of college in digs off the Iffley Road: to be
precise, a council house kept by Harry and Edith Walford. It
was late October. Eddie had just completed the running-in of his
new M.G. Midget, and he arranged to bring it up from Walsall
to the works at Abingdon for its first service. Naturally he called
for me. In fact he called for breakfast.

It was a finely-drizzly morning after a long dry spell; the
tarmac roads were at their most treacherous. But Eddie was full
of joy in the superlative road-holding and cornering of his new
car. After the Morgan, that is. He related with gusto how on the
way down he had passed a Riley Gamecock going in the opposite direction. They were both, he guessed, doing 70 – so the
combined speed as they passed, on the rather narrow road, was
140 m.p.h. Eddie enjoyed calculations and speculations of that
order. One day as we lay on our backs in a meadow, enjoying
the sun while we rested from the non-existent fishing, he had
entertained me with calculations and speculations about the
nature of the physical universe – finite or infinite? – which told
me that he had a first-rate brain that would have responded

brilliantly to training. He never accepted truisms or platitudes as facts until he had examined them in the light of his intelligence and experience and found them plausible.

Eddie arrived, after his 70-mile trip, at eight o'clock. At about half-past or a little later we set off for Abingdon. On a long, long wet bend on the outskirts of the city we went into an uncontrollable skid. Eddie had just mentioned to me that we were doing sixty and wasn't she sweet?

The car turned round and shot backwards under the back of a huge old lorry parked at the kerb, heavily laden with bricks. A five-tonner. Everything seemed to take an awful long time; it was as if this were a slow-motion film unrolling. I had plenty of time to register the fact that the day went quite dark as we slipped underneath the vast overhang of the truck. One of the pointed rear wings of the car punctured one of the vast rear tyres of the lorry. I was grasping the top corner of the metal-framed windscreen with my left hand, with the arm bent and rigid, and my left elbow came into contact with one of the chassis members, end-on. From which point of contact the effort was applied, I do not know; but the impact shifted that laden lorry, which had the brakes on, six feet.

There must have been a considerable noise to bring all those people running and shouting, but I wasn't aware of it. We were sitting there, side by side, nice and snug as one was in the old J2 Midget, it was a bit dark, and very quiet. I turned to see if Eddie was OK. He looked OK.

'I'm all right, Eddie. How are you?' I asked.

He smiled a great smile of relief and hopped out, and drew me out after him. Later he told me that he was very pleased indeed to hear me say that. He thought it was a nice thing to say.

I still cannot straighten my left arm properly, though I think it's getting better.

We took the M.G. into the works on a lorry. When they had rebuilt it – and done that first service – Eddie came up again to collect it. The crankshaft broke as he was trundling through Oxford at 25 m.p.h. This time he had it painted black while they were at it: I think he had been persuaded that green was an unlucky colour. He collected his black car and wrapped it around a lamp post on the outskirts of Wolverhampton.

Nowadays Eddie and I drive sedate family cars sedately.

But if you don't remember what you were like when you were young, your memory is dangerously defective.

It isn't only the wild bohemians who are generous, you know. I've known all sorts, some generous bohemians and some right twisters, scroungers, parasites. Eddie is, I suppose, the epitome of bourgeois conservatism, in a quiet way: local butcher, member of the golf club, drives a Wolseley. But how absurd these tags and labels and categories are. I don't think I ever knew a more generous man. His mother was a very sweet lady, a real darling. Much later on in life, when I had been absent from the scene for many years, she told me on the quiet, but with pride, of the good works Eddie did by stealth. It was the only department of his life in which stealth figured.

Dear stalwart friend, you have been closer to me, throughout the vicissitudes of my life, than ever you suspected.

8

Jim's Jungle

JIM BEALE'S voice was the authentic voice of journalism, in the sense that it was the first voice I ever heard, actually speaking to me personally, from a newspaper office. It was a very impressive voice, somehow crisp yet deep. This was just as it should be, for Jim was the telephonist at the *Birmingham Gazette* and *Evening Despatch*.

The telephonist, the one and only. Jim sat all day at his little switchboard in his cubby-hole by the back stairs on the third floor – sorry, Third Floor – of Newspaper House, just off Corporation Street, whipping the plugs in and out like a good 'un. He was a master of his craft and never put a foot or a plug wrong in all the years I knew him. And he could charm the hind legs off a brass pot.

So it was Jim whose voice I heard when I put through my call to Mr T. J. Taylor, the Circulation Manager. Jim had such an acute ear for a telephone voice that he effortlessly and instantly recognised mine when he next heard it a week or so later; I having in the meantime talked my way past Mr Taylor, to whom I had the most tenuous of introductions, talked my way into the well-protected heart of Mr T. T. Stanley, the

Managing Editor who ran the whole editorial side, and landed myself a month's trial without pay as a learner-reporter. The first time I lifted a phone in the reporters' room to make my positive first call as a cub, Jim recognised my voice.

'Hello,' he said, 'so you made it. Congratulations.'

It occurred to me later that Jim might just conceivably have caught odd scraps of the passionate tirade I put over to T. J. Taylor. I wouldn't accuse him of listening-in, though. He wouldn't like that. But it was a fact that Jim knew everything that was going on. He was the best-informed man on the staff. He had more news under his hat than the Chief Reporter. If we'd printed Jim's news we might have made it a more interesting paper.

Invited along, I visited Jim straightaway and discovered what a rare nice chap he was and what a lovely little refuge he had there in his little cubby-hole. There was a spare telephone there, and a chair, and quite a few of us formed a habit of making all our calls, business and pleasure, from Jim's place. No wonder he was a well-informed man.

He was a big, ruddy-faced, dark-haired man, running to fat, who had lost a leg in the Great War, in which he had been a sergeant-major and I can just imagine it. Tough, shrewd, genial, fascinated by the goings-on, Jim had the insatiable curiosity of a first-class reporter and the discretion, the tact, of a first-rate bishop's chaplain. He was father-confessor to all the young reporters and he never told tales. His judgment of character was superb. Naturally, being what he was, a good fellow, he had a weakness for the weaker brethren among us, the sinners and renegades; the back-sliders, the borrowers (not that anyone ever touched Jim); the chronic broke, the incipient drunkards, the girl-happy, the rebellious, the scatty, the human. Not that he adopted any moral postures, though he occasionally offered sound advice. But he was simply this rare and beautiful thing, an observer in a perfect position to observe, fascinated by the quiddity of his companions, the barminess of the world in which he worked. He had an exceedingly shrewd gift of prophecy so far as pro-motion and demotion went. He had observed men in competition all his life and he knew who had what it took to rise or fall. His humour, unfailing, was sardonic, almost cynical. He was grand company.

You may think that, having only one lame telephonist instead of a great battery of birds, we were a small-time outfit; but not so. It was a fine modern office and a big progressive firm. It never came to very much, owing perhaps to the ineffable (but much eff'd) carefulness in money matters of the proprietors, Westminster Press Provincial Newspapers Ltd, successors to the Starmer Group. This prudent bunch, infested by Quakers and cocoa moguls, professed high Liberal principles but paid no more than they could get away with. They owned a lot of good papers and plant up and down the country and employed a lot of good journalists from time to time. But of course they couldn't keep them. The good ones escaped to Fleet Street or the *Birmingham Post* and *Mail* as soon as they had learned their trade. The present editor of *The Sunday Times*, Harold Evans, tells me that things have changed since my days in Birmingham. He was editor of the group's Darlington *Northern Echo*, twenty years later, and he says the pay was quite normal then. I notice he still left for Fleet Street. But I accept his word for it – I'd accept his word for anything. All I'm saying is that in the mid-Thirties when I was a bright young boyo they were as tight as Jim Callaghan's smile.

With the talent they had around, and the plant and facilities, even allowing for Jim's one-man telephone exchange, they had enough on the ball to have seen the opposition right off the streets. The opposition consisted mainly of the *Birmingham* (morning) *Post* and (evening) *Mail*, plus a certain amount of combat from the *Wolverhampton Express and Star* in the Black Country areas. All those papers were very dull. Virtuous, I don't doubt it, but not very bright. The *Post* and *Mail* were great dreary slabby things belonging to, at the very latest, the Joseph Chamberlain era; Tory to the last euphemism, devoted to the great heart-warming cause summed up in those immortal lines *Ho the rich gets richer and the poor gets poorer*. They actually employed some very good writers, some outstandingly judicious and elegant critics, some utterly reliable reporters. They rarely printed misprints. Solid, comprehensive, dependable, in a negative sort of way, they were good sound Tory papers of another age, and as dull as the Chamberlain family itself. The *Express and Star* was just a mess, really provincial in the worst sense.

We should have been able to see that lot off, but we never

began to, and after all the years of battle we lost out not long after the war – long after I had left, let me say, just as if it made a difference – and were duly merged with the *Post* and *Mail*. I hasten to add that nowadays the *Post* and *Mail* are utterly transformed, and so for that matter is the *Express and Star*. Unrecognisably. They are now, and especially the Birmingham pair, first-rate examples of the liveliest and best in provincial journalism. Which only really means that they have nearly everything except that little element of calculated outrage which marks the real leaders in national and international journalism.

But to get back to the hominids infesting Jim Beale's private jungle.... There were some unforgettable characters around, I must say. To prove it, I haven't forgotten them, and it's going on for forty years now, heaven help us. To be precise, it was in 1934 that I joined the party, at twenty-one, and I am writing now in 1972, at fifty-nine. And not writing any better, either. But what can you expect, after more than ten million words?

In his sardonically avuncular way, Jim presided over the springtime of quite a number of young journalists who were to become mildly notorious, or if you like famous, after leaving Newspaper House. Don Iddon, later to become the celebrated New York Correspondent of the *Daily Mail*, was the leading figure when I arrived. His real name was Ernest Frederick Iddon. He signed his pieces E.F.I., in 8-point Doric caps, and thought that made him famous. The first thing he did when we met was to take me along to the library and show me all his 'signed' reports and features on the files. Don liked you to know that he was somebody. He *was* somebody; he was the personality he had devised to match his dreams and mask his shortcomings. The only serious shortcoming was his reluctance to face the fact that he could not take anything or anybody really seriously, except the dream persona, Don Iddon, to which he was devoted with that rare singleness of purpose that makes people become what they most want to become.

Don was the first really flamboyant 'personality', in the modern sense of someone who projects an image, that I had met; or perhaps I should say recognised. Of course life is and always was full of them, but they were thin on the ground in the Black Country, where the prevailing ethos was against ebullient display of ego – you had to mask it as something else to get away with it, you had to play down the personal ego a bit and mask it with an assumed persona that had little relation to the real or inner one. We accepted 'character' but suspected 'personality'. Don's personality, as amended by his own efforts on the basis of a natural style, was wholly delightful once you got over the slight shock of meeting such outrageous, unashamed egotism.

He was quite free of the sanctimonious hypocrisy which affected some of us. He not only admitted his faults and short-comings, but advertised them with a refreshing candour. Alone among my acquaintance up to date, he candidly confessed his ruthless ambitions. He was going to get to the top, and not up the back stairs, either. He frankly loved ostentation, luxury and swank. He had chosen journalism because it gave a *young* man the chance to make good money and live a glamorous life at one and the same time. Don came from Lancashire and had his full share of the legendary hard-headed shrewdness of that area, he put a high value on money and ostentation, he affected from time to time to have a comprehensive personal knowledge of the industrial working classes and their psychology, but actually he could not wait to leave them behind. Like Granada cynically exploiting sentimental nostalgia and working class *mores* in *Coronation Street*, Don could play the bluff northerner part when it suited him. But in fact he did not give much of his attention to the sufferings of the proletariat, which at that time was suffer-ing quite somewhat. He was a middle-class lad who was getting on and going up and although he paid fairly regular duty visits to the old folks he always hurried back. Birmingham was only the first stop on the way South, to the great metropolis where a smart lad could get away with almost anything.

The lovable thing about Don was that he was likely to break down in the middle of some great pompous tirade about his professional patriotic ideals – England, *his* England – and laugh at himself. 'Go on, then, hit me,' he would invite sundry fellow members of the Press Club, whom he had infuriated to the point of mayhem by his unbridled candour. He would offer his chubby chin to the fists of his enraged inquisitors. But no one ever did hit him. How could you? You might in your stuffy way think him a great poseur, but you had to admit that he was not only the most entertaining character in sight but actually a man of considerable honesty. (I'm not suggesting that he was *not* patriotic, you understand. He was. But professionally as well as privately.)

Don was actually a good reporter; in some respects, a very good one. He could turn his hand to a lot of things; cover a murder case or a football game, cope with coppers, dig a human story out of some poor spavined wretch, write rousing personal features, interview the celebrated very ably. He had a real talent, the limitations of which he knew perfectly well, and onto his talent he superimposed this carefully constructed personal life-style, as we call it nowadays, which was very shrewdly conceived because it really did correspond to those actual elements in his psychological make-up which he liked most. Come to think, this is a quite rational way of adjusting your *given* personality. Some of us accept the humiliated image which others are only too happy to assign to us; some, like Don, brush aside the bits they don't like and concentrate on strengthening the bits they do. Why not?

Ebullience, flamboyance, glamour, a touch of cheerful outrage – that was our Don. In person he was a chubby, pink-faced boy, not quite so tall as he would have liked, well-made if a shade plump, with straight brown hair which he kept carefully slick, too small a nose, a full-lipped mouth that was rarely shut, and nice brown eyes usually wide open in simulated outrage or innocence. He was our snappiest dresser. He spent more than anyone else would dream of spending on clothes, always well-made, conservative yet just touched with dash. The good blue suits, cream silk shirts and board-room ties, were set off by something slightly *outré* in the curling brim of the good brown trilby, something a shade dashing in the overcoat and shoes.

To offset his expenses he held periodical auctions of his un-wanted clothes, in the reporters' room. These were always well-publicised – everything Don did was well publicised – and well attended. I got a fine black leather motoring coat for a pound, that way, which later in a fit of absent-mindedness, having changed momentarily (but, as I thought, permanently) from an open car to a saloon, I sold, also for £1, to the chief sub-editor of the *Despatch*. Don was a natural auctioneer and rarely had anything left on his hands. He would have done well in almost any branch of human activity which put a premium on out-going flamboyance, personal dash and the gift of the gab. He enjoyed himself enormously, and naturally other people enjoyed him too. Several disapproved of him, from time to time, and more affected to find him a joke, but no one ever ignored him.

I was far from impressed when, on meeting me, he took me to the files to dazzle me with his brilliance and importance. But within a day or two we were good friends. Something Don said, within that first week, not only endeared him to me, but revealed a great deal about his make-up.

'As soon as I heard you were coming,' he said, 'with all those Oxford degrees and so on, I realised I had to do one of two things right away. I had to over-awe you from the start, or come to an accommodation with you. There's only room for one star turn here.'

As soon as he realised that far from being over-awed, I was amused and entertained by his personality, he capitulated in that disarming way of his, and we became fast friends, or as fast as friends could be in that competitive atmosphere. Don realised, as he admitted, that while I had certain talents for the game, I also had an unaggressive personality and was no threat to his personal ascendancy as our leading young lion. I used to prick his pomp from time to time with unkind shots of cynical intuition, but oftener I took pleasure in egging him on, aiding and abetting the flowering of his ego. For in a rather unamusing town, he gave a lot of simple pleasure.

He drove the most dashing car in the business, a long low Standard Avon two-seater, which had no performance at all but was shrewdly designed to look as if it had. It's not surprising that Don was the first among us to own the new-fangled Jaguar or Jew's Bentley when it burst upon the scene. Don was one of nature's Jag types. It was because Lord Lyons knew that there were a lot of people with Don's psychology just waiting for the Jaguar that he designed it, and succeeded with it, and deserved to.

Don did not live in digs like any other young reporter away from home. He lived in a *private hotel*, somewhere out in the suburban wilds of Erdington, where he impressed the other boarders – all professional people – with the dazzle of his glamour and panache. I remember him saying to me one lovely morning when we had slipped out for a quick coffee in the Kardomah:

'There I was driving along this morning, from my hotel to

my office, wearing a *good* suit, smoking a *good* cigarette, driving a *good* car....'

There were about two million unemployed at the time.

There was a charming childish openness about this frank joy in his success, his glamour, his brilliance. You couldn't resent it. Well, I couldn't. Though in some ways Don incarnated attitudes of which I was only too ready to disapprove – what later became known as the Room At The Top approach: go-getting materialism, rat racing – yet because he made a game of it, because he was essentially an actor unabashedly playing his favourite role, Don Iddon, Ace Reporter, and playing it with such zest and style and with a twinkle in his eye – for all these reasons, and for the simple reason that he was basically a limited, shrewd, fun-loving lad who understood perfectly his own limitations and was determined to push his luck as far as it would go, with his tongue in his cheek.... Well, I just liked the lad, his company was a joy. You had to take him with a pinch of salt, deflate him a bit when he got *too* outrageously cocky, but enjoy the act along with its most appreciative fan, Ernest Frederick himself.

We never called him Ernest, or Frederick, or Don. The 'Don' part he invented after he had joined the *Daily Mail*. To us he was Id, or the Id. Both Id and Ego: perhaps the only time they were one and the same thing. I was able to help him materially, for very soon after entering the trade, nine months in fact to the day, a rather premature pregnancy ended and I was appointed Features Editor of the *Evening Despatch*. Thereafter, playing my own favourite game of layout and display – the only part of the newspaper game which never palled – I was able to 'feature' Id, and indeed the rest of my friends and colleagues, giving them bigger by-lines, more extravagant promotion, than ever they had enjoyed in the costive days which preceded this gay era on which we now embarked.

I arbitrarily settled on 24-point type as being the biggest I would allow anyone's name to appear in, except my own. That is a third of an inch tall, enormous by the standards of my predecessors, who had not only paid careful money but also screwed down every incipient sign of personality, grudgingly awarding 8-point Doric black initials at the end of a story as something of an accolade, and a 10- or 12-point light-faced by-line as something quite sensational.

Now we went mad, encouraged by the example of the *Daily Express*, which was just coming to its historic (and histrionic) peak under the editorship of Arthur Christiansen. He gave free rein to two brilliant layout men, John Rayner and Harold Keeble, both daring innovators. There were then three distinctive styles in Fleet Street: the *Express*, the *News Chronicle*, and the *Mirror*. I warmed to the *Express* style, finding the *Mirror* too blatantly vulgar and the *News Chronicle*, though beautiful, too austere. None of the other papers had anything much to say to me. The *Express* was warm, vital, exciting. We would be warm, vital and exciting too.

We duly became all those things, but with one little difference. Our vivacity was mainly visual. I don't say we didn't publish some good words from time to time – there were plenty of good writers and ideas men around – but I'm speaking mainly from the viewpoint of the Features Editor and he had to manage on the most attenuated budget. All those lively lads were reporters; there were no feature writers as such, and anything they did for me they did in their own time, for the princely reward of three-halfpence a line. It doesn't bring the best out of a chap who has slogged all day for the Chief Reporter. My usual fee to an outside contributor was, reckoned on the same lavish basis, about a guinea, sometimes as much as thirty bob. You don't attract the best talent that way, do you? So it was mainly super-ficial excitement, visual fireworks. I don't think the readers cared any too much about the visual fireworks. But the lads saw their names in anything up to 24-point Chelt. Bold caps or Old Face Heavy or Gill Sans or Metro Black, and they were quite excited, even if the readers weren't.

And none more so than Ernest Frederick Don Iddon from Preston, Lancs.

Don was certainly the most emphatic personality in Jim's jungle, and he was by far the best attuned to the wavelength of success in that particular field. He went farthest and fastest, earned more money and glory than any of us. He talked himself into bigger jobs – but, be it said, he held them down. The climate of journalism has changed, of course, but I do not doubt that much the same qualities of personal flamboyance and sparkling self-confidence still help an aspirant.

Don worshipped success, the bitch goddess, and she smiled on him, as she smiles on all who worship her sincerely. It is a form of sincerity that cannot be counterfeited. I have known a good many success-worshippers, including a fair proportion of eager beavers, go-getters, rat-racers, phoneys, creeps; but Don had a quality that set him aside from all that sort. There was a sort of innocence in his pursuit of the bitch. He was truly sincere, he truly loved her. He gloried in his snobbery. He played the part loving every moment of it, laughing at himself, applauding himself; always some likeable part of himself standing aside, in the wings, looking on, and laughing. With Don, it really *was* an act, an act of which he never tired, which never ossified into the only reality. An act; he never tried to kid us otherwise. His pomposity was put on, and to his enormous credit, it remained an assumed pomposity, a joke which he enjoyed as much as anyone. He was an actor whose performance enchanted himself, and if others were taken in by it, so much the better; but you didn't have to be taken in, and if you weren't, no hard feelings. Of all the climbers I have known, and I've known some, Don was the most endearing. The most entertaining. And in a sense which some will understand, some won't, the most honest.

The other outstanding character in Jim's jungle was our editor, Harold Benoit. I have worked for many editors in my time, including the best in the world, and Ben was one of the three or four most remarkable. As it happens he never left Birmingham, but he could easily have become a celebrated figure in Fleet Street had he so chosen. He had been a very talented chief sub-editor of the *Gazette*, with a flair for the dramatics of the front page. The front page is a theatre, or at any rate a stage; the masthead a proscenium arch beneath which the mute and frozen choreography of design presents the crazy play of life arrested in a moment of maximum significance and drama. A good front-page designer is an impresario who works without rehearsal, using the players wished upon him by the caprice of fate, some stars, some stumblebums; working from a script that is still being written and re-written during the performance, a palimpsest which has to be seized and interpreted during the brief moment when it is visible, before it is over-written by the next.

The very best front-page men have the faculty of living in two dimensions at once. On one hand, finely attuned to the flux and flow of events, aware as if by a sixth sense of the trend events are taking, capable of interpreting and evaluating almost instantaneously the relative significance of the components of the inchoate flux. On the other hand, stable; rooted in what I can only call the *apparent historic permanence of the evaluated moment* – a quality of a rare kind, a truly theatrical quality, which makes its possessor capable of expressing his decision in graphic terms, in terms of a visual sensibility which in the very act of freezing the evaluated moment, irresistibly suggests movement, unfolding, a dynamic continuing process. Every front page as it is sent away to the printer is in theatrical terms a curtain – but not only a curtain falling, also a curtain rising. I know no work that calls for such diverse and apparently contradictory qualities in a man. It is at once exhausting and exhilarating. Making a great front page is a work of art – op art and pop art included. Its very ephemerality makes it irresistibly fascinating to a certain temperament.

Ben (like my present Editor, Harold Evans of *The Sunday Times*) possessed this quality to a considerable degree. If Ben fell short of the very highest standard, it was because his appreciation of typography was ever so slightly defective; he did not quite have the scholarship and the aesthetic sensibility of the very finest typographers. But we are talking in quibbles: in his day, weight for weight, he was quite outstanding, and his pages possessed a vitality and exuberance which made him a marked man in our little world of graphic histrionics. He was appointed editor of the *Evening Despatch* shortly after my arrival on the scene, and almost his first rash act was to appoint me his Features Editor. I shared his room, his confidence and his friendship for five miraculous years, the happiest years of my working life. I cannot calculate my debt to him.

His chief benefaction was that he set me free to find my own way around. It may seem a negative contribution, put in that austere yet precise manner. In fact it was precisely the contribution which I needed. Ben actually taught me a great deal, of course; no one could have been more forthcoming, painstaking and assiduous. But the important element in our association was trust and freedom. By giving me my head, he inspired me with confidence in my talent. I was, after all, an exceedingly new newcomer to the trade. By making me an executive and giving me a really free hand, Ben made me at a stroke responsible, confident and adventurous.

His confidence in me released those better qualities which authoritarian repression always stifles. I changed almost overnight, from a rather harum-scarum bohemian reporter and feature writer into a positively dedicated production executive with a vengeance, passionately devoted to my pages. I was literally in love with my job. I poured more creativity into those pages than into homemaking, political thought, patriotism, or any leisure pursuit. I can quite see now that this was disproportionate, but that is how it was. I clocked in at eight o'clock sharp, did a day's work which would kill me now, sometimes in time of crisis worked straight through two days and a night without leaving my office, except for a quick snack and drink.

I had many interests, some of them very vivid, but nothing in the world outside could compete in fascination with this heavenly job of editing features, making up those beautiful big dramatic pages. I did the job for relatively little pay, though my rises came steadily, and had I not got married and fallen in love also with motor cars I should hardly have noticed the need for money. From the age of twenty-one to twenty-six, when I left for Fleet Street, the *Daily Express*, I enjoyed more creative 'job satisfaction' than at any other time of my life. I owe this mainly to Ben and I want him to know that I acknowledge the debt. At seventy-three he is still living an active life in Shropshire, out of the business but absorbed in growing clematis and other fine plants, still 'thinking big', white-haired now but otherwise virtually unchanged from when I knew him first.

Ben was a great believer in 'thinking big'. He was (and in fact he still is) a barrel-chested man of medium height, who held himself erect and moved briskly, rather like a soldier. He had been a soldier. He had a squarish head and face and a very square jaw, was clean-shaven and in every way spruce and well-turned-out. He had a fairly prominent peaky nose, just like Edward Heath's. I have seen it on several ambitious men. Ben looked smart and moved smartly, throwing back his shoulders and hurrying along at the pace of the light infantry, even if he was only going from our joint office down the corridor to the sub's room or the heads. No one remained unaware of Ben. He had presence, he held himself well, as the phrase goes, carried himself well. He was both stiff and springy. He wore double-breasted lounge suits, immaculately pressed. Don was the first of us to own a Jaguar, but not until he had left for Fleet Street. Ben was the first journalist to own a Jaguar in Birmingham. I road-tested it for him (it was slightly second-hand). Black, of course, with tan hide: what else, for a go-ahead executive? It completed the picture.

That Ben could afford a Jaguar indicates that the Group paid its top executives well, even if they economised on the 'lower echelons' or p.b.i. Actually, I suspect, you got what you stuck out for, to a certain extent and providing it wasn't much. For example, when the *Daily Express* first offered me ten guineas (£10.50) a week (I was earning £6.75 as features editor) the Group countered with an offer of eight guineas (£8.40). Which I accepted. *Pro tem.* Ben fought to get me the full ten which the *Express* had offered, but reported to me that the general manager shrewdly observed, 'He can live as well on eight in Birmingham as he would on ten in London.' Perfectly true, but indicating a certain type of thinking. I must say the rise of 33 shillings a week seemed the most prodigious thing that had happened to us since the invention of pay. We instantly went in hock for an Export model Austin Ruby. That looked after the rise quite well, or most of it.

Ben smoked Senior Service, I smoked Players (or Erinmore in my pipe when I was feeling pipe-ish, that is to say steady, dependable, calm) and Mrs Luck from the canteen turned up at regular intervals with the tea and buns. At lunch time and after work we nipped into the pub on the corner and settled down to a few sticks of mild or bitter. The stick was a Brummagem measure; perhaps it existed elsewhere, but I don't know. It was a nefarious, insidious measure. It was less than half a pint but perhaps a little more than a gill. It cost about twopence, perhaps twopence-ha'penny. Drinkers who were reluctant to become drunkards, or to admit to themselves that they were already drunkards, used to drink sticks, under the impression that they were hardly drinking at all. Of course it was just like Woodbines, Stars, Weights, and De Reszke Minors: once hooked, you consumed a prodigious quantity without ever really having a good drink (or smoke). Each stick was such a pissy little apology for a drink, in itself: how could you possibly be accused of being a boozer, with a tiddly little thing like that in your hand? Little drops of water, little grains of sand.... Occasionally I used to rebel against the prudential hypocrisy of the stick and order outrageous pints. Ben shook his head.

Ben left the daily running of the paper to three of us. I ran the third of it devoted to features, Mr Gillman was chief sub-editor and ran the news pages, and Mr Norman was sports editor. Two men and a boy. But though Ben rarely interfered with today's paper, he was always busy planning next year's. This was his long suit: far-sightedness. Harold Evans once told me that the chief strain of editing *The Sunday Times* was that he was working on two papers at once – editing this week's issue and trying to visualise the paper as it should be five years ahead, or two years ahead. It must be murderous. Ben preserved his youthful energy and drive, perhaps, because he let us under-lings get on with today's paper and concentrated much of his abundant energy on next year's. He was always very much on the job, available for consultation, missing nothing: don't get me wrong. But having appointed his executives, and laid down the lines on which he wanted the paper to be edited, he did have this marvellous gift of letting us get on with it, while he brooded about the future and how to make silk purses out of sows' ears.

He was always battling with the management for more money, bigger papers, more staff – that of sort of long-term politicking which always sent me sound asleep. I don't know why. I could only enjoy the concrete, immediate, ephemeral job of my pages. I was aware of, in fact highly sensitive to, the climate and atmosphere of journalism, always inventing new styles, gimmicks, visual jokes, and all that heavenly sort of stuff. I was very happy indeed to leave it to Ben to cope with the high-level executive job, for which he was perfectly cut out, and I not at all. So everyone was happy.

If I have learned anything from my thirty-seven years in journalism, it is that nothing fails like success – in this particular sense, that bright young journalists are always being promoted beyond their true capacities. It has happened to me, and I admit it, I admitted it at the time. And I've seen it happen to quite a few chaps: excellent sub-editors promoted out of their depth to executive rank, where they flounder: good reporters and feature writers promoted to columnist, where they lose touch. I have known only three actual *editors* who would have been both happier and more effective if they had remained assistant editors, or feature editors, or chief sub-editors: but below that dizzy rank, in the ranks of the senior executives, I've known quite several who never 'lived up to their promise' for the simple reason that they had reached their peak in their more humble posts, and simply did not function effectively when raised up into another sphere of activity.

Of course you can't blame anybody, and I don't. It's natural. But sad. I personally was one of nature's features editors, or to be more precise, one of nature's subs, a display man, layout man, typographer, designer, re-write man, headline writer, caption writer – that sort of really down-to-earth activity, which was and is profoundly exciting and satisfying, was really all I wanted, it was the limit of my creativity and I should have been quite happy to stick with it. And I had no notion of 'man management': I don't like managing men. But of course when you're offered promotion you tend to take it, and your bosses tend to see you 'developing' in ways which, though no one is to know it, you are not fitted to develop. Of course there have been a lot of great versatile journalists who have gone through *all* the stages brilliantly, developing and maturing and becoming first-rate executives, yea, even up to editors and chief executives.

So it was all right. Ben thought big, thought ahead. I soldiered on happily drawing my big beautiful designs (well, I thought they were beautiful, which was what counted in terms of happiness). They were certainly dramatic, and vivacious. Life itself was dramatic and vivacious. In the office we toiled, nay, slaved; in the pub we conducted fierce unsparing inquests on the day's editions, looked ahead to the morrow, and listened to Ben looking ahead to the morrow's many morrows. A field which he had to himself, and luxuriated in. I was happy that there *was* a literal tomorrow, in which the whole rackety exhausting business could be gone through yet again, new permutations, the stimulus of serendipity, happening upon new ideas like a goldminer picking and shovelling away, confident that there's still gold in them thar hills, not quite sure how it will turn out but sure it *will*. It was the ephemerality of the game, I think, which made me so happy – what else could have suited so well my mercurial temperament? Until bedtime, though, I was happy about today's little lot: I loved this moment of pause and fulfilment. I cherished it, rested upon it, drew joy and strength and courage from it, to the last possible moment when today turns into tomorrow and you have to face the fact that the dead shall bury the dead and all's to do again.

You have to have the temperament for it.

To Ben, it was already dead meat, and tomorrow was too near, too sure to be rather like today. His mind ranged ahead, browsing in pastures which I could scarcely imagine, and hardly wanted to. He was a great editor, Ben, and in his way a great man. Totally consistent, more consistent than almost anyone I have known in the business, he never faltered, never rested, never flinched from the battle. He was loyalty itself to his men, looked after us like brothers and sons, fought to improve our lot, infused us with pride in our paper and our craft, bashed us when bashing was called for. Before I left Birmingham for Fleet Street, he had been appointed Editor-in-Chief of the *Gazette* and *Despatch*. His rise was like a straight line on a graph. He retained the respect and affection of a lot of journalists, though he could be ferocious when ferocity was called for. But it was always man-to-man; never *de haut en bas*. His heart was kind and generous. He was an inspiration to work for. If our papers never quite broke through and won that battle which he fought against the local opposition with such singleness of purpose, such dedication and tenacity, it was not his fault. I suspect it was something to do with our wishy-washy political stance and something to do with the curious economics of the trade. I notice that the *Post* and *Mail*, when they had absorbed us and Ben had left the scene, adopted what was liveliest and most vivacious in us and welded it to their own superior stability, to make a new product better than either of the old.

The present brilliantly successful Editor of the *Birmingham Mail*, my old friend and colleague Frank Owens, CBE, began his reporting career in Birmingham under Harold Benoit.

So did a lot of fine fellows whom I am proud and happy to recall. Some have vanished from my ken; some remain friends even if we rarely meet. Roland Hurman, Industrial Editor of the *Daily Mail*, assistant editor of the *Daily Mirror*, and now Associate Editor of the *Daily Express*. Norman Shrapnel, parliamentary sketch writer for the *Guardian*, a man so brilliant he could have become almost anything in the writing line. Jo Adams, who was at Saint Catherine's, Oxford, with me, and for years my closest, most intimate friend, who became a London film critic on the *Star* and *News* and also worked for the *Evening Standard*. Grahame Stanford, columnist of the *News of the World*. Ray 'Boyo' Hill, still in Birmingham as correspondent of the *Mirror*; a great character Ray. Maurice Cheesewright. Reeves Quann. The brilliant Ivan Roe, brainiest of us all, and by far, though not necessarily for that reason, the most successful in material terms. Young Frank Hardaker who went to Canada, and buoyant, elegant Kenneth Bolton who went to Kenya. Dear old pals, I salute you all. But it's time to leave Jim's Jungle and head for the Big Smoke, where fiercer beasties, the real man-eaters, prowl.

9

Neb and Neb's Ma

NEB really belongs in the section which I have called Jim's Jungle: he was a fully paid-up member of the mythology in those halcyon days in Birmingham when nothing seemed impossible. But I cannot leave Neb as one among several; he was more than just a journalistic colleague. He was a friend whose life became entwined with our lives.

Neb's real name is Ronald Neibour, but he has always been known, professionally and among his friends, as Neb. He is a cartoonist whose work you may remember from his days on the *Daily Mail* and the London *Evening News*. His speciality was the pocket cartoon. There are lots of them now, it's an art form which has great appeal; Neb was in there in the early days of the *genre*. He is retired now, and lives in Malaga, Spain.

I found him in the library of the Birmingham *Evening Despatch* shortly after I had been appointed Features Editor of that newspaper. I found him sitting there at a littered table near the window, re-touching photographs, and looking rather like a Saint Bernard which had lost the cask. He had reason to be somewhat dejected. He had been 'transferred' (in the footballer's sense of the word) from an Oxford paper; but having been obtained, he was not being used. He showed me some of his comic drawings and I was filled, nay suffused, with that holy righteousness that suffuses impresarios when they discover real talent being hidden or perverted or thwarted or frustrated. With a pure sort of selfless joy – how rare that feeling is – I liberated him forthwith from those dreary chores – touching up photographs, indeed – and set him to work decorating my feature pages with every imaginable kind of vivacious and charming fancy, both great and small. Of course I was pickling a rod for my own back; sooner or later his work was bound to be spotted in Fleet Street and bags of gold dangled before his dreamy eyes. And so it came about.

But for a few years, or at any rate a year or two, Neb was my right-hand man and close companion, drawing away marvellously; and even when he departed for the *Daily Mail*, we remained closely in touch, and the friendship was resumed as if it had never been interrupted when I went to the *Daily Express*. Nowadays we rarely meet, but when contact is made, it is always as if we had parted only yesterday. This is friendship.

Neb was about six feet six inches tall, and a big man in every way. I don't know how it is now, since he had pneumonia in Sunny Spain, but he used to pack a fair wallop in either hand, though fortunately he was a swinger and you know how it is with these round-arm punchers, they miss as often as they connect and half the power of the blow is dissipated anyway, it takes such a long way round. This was just as well because if he had punched his weight, with straight short punches, I doubt if I'd have survived it. For we were always sparring. Neb was a friend of Jack Petersen, the heavyweight champion of Great Britain; he had lived in Barry himself; we were both keen on the noble and brutal art. But our sparring began, actually, as a means of getting a bit of work done.

Neb liked to take his own time over a job. I wanted it done in my time, which was usually yesterday, or at least half an hour ago. So I used to sink a hook into the ribs to see how that affected his speed. It did! Neb could take a lot of punishment, but when sufficiently aroused, he would rise like a great shaggy bear and chase me out of the library, down the corridor and into the Gents, where, cornered, I would have to take a heavy swing or three.

It was a case of One-Round Wiggin all over again. I always

enjoyed boxing, and was quite good at it for one round, but my physique told against me. As often as not I was all over my opponent in the first round, scoring freely with a nice straight left and perhaps getting across with a telling right. But if I didn't win in the first, I was pretty sure to lose in the second. One busy round usually exhausted me, in the second I could hardly hold my thin arms up, and since I had a glass chin as well, it was odds on curtains. Fortunately Neb was a character with great forbearance and compassion and if he knocked me down, he also picked me up.

On particularly good creative days we used to get home black and blue. 'Look at your arms!' my wife would cry. And Neb's ma complained bitterly about the colour of his ribs. I don't think this production system was current in many creative offices.

Neb's ma was a wonderful character. She was inclined to be secretive about her age but she was certainly well into her eighties when she died, having chain-smoked Players Weights throughout her adult life. She had the radio on all day, always ever so slightly off-tune, not because she approved of what was being said, but because she enjoyed disapproving of it. She would lie back in the old armchair by the fire with a Weight dangling from her lips, and her eyes closed, resting from the chores of the day. We used to nudge each other and jerk a thumb, watching with fascination to see if she would wake up before the cigarette burned her lips or if somebody would have to sneak over and remove it. She always won. Just when you were sure that she was sound asleep – 'Rubbish!' she would say, 'Load of nonsense.'

I've often thought that if broadcasters, I mean television broadcasters as well as radio, of course, could hear what people said to them during their little spiels they wouldn't be quite so complacent. In fact they couldn't do it at all. When occasionally someone would say to me that I was a bit rough, as a critic, I used to think my goodness, you should see my mail. It's the unpaid critics, the amateurs, who really get stuck in. Of course they've no inhibitions about the law of libel, for one thing.

I noticed over the years, when I was a critic, that people wrote to me comparatively rarely to complain that I had been too severe: far oftener they wrote to complain, in withering terms, that I had been much too indulgent. Being a television critic is a funny job, of which eventually I tired, but although some critics obviously enjoy using the knife and inflating their own egos by deflating others', on the whole I find professional critics rather more, not less, temperate and judicious than amateurs – judging from my mail and the comments I have heard. A good pro will always try to relate what he has seen to some general standard, some larger body of work by which it may properly be judged. True, there are some vicious assassins who are only in love with themselves, and really enjoy putting the blade in. The good critic really enjoys sharing pleasure – but it's a good deal harder to write a piece of praise of someone's work, and make it interesting to read, than to bring down the hammer on the anvil with a showy display of sparks.

Neb's ma was one of nature's critics. She had a lovely mordant sense of humour, what I have come to consider a typically Cockney approach, though I dare say you find it everywhere, to greater or less degree. She liked to pose as a thorough-going cynic, though in fact she had the kindest heart you could wish to find. She was very sceptical of claims and assumptions, especially if it was virtue that was being assumed. For politicians she had no time at all, which spoke well for her sagacity; but she maintained her sceptical front to all who tried to 'come it across' her, whether it were the baker with his forecast of fresher bread tomorrow, the milkman with his excuses for forgetting the yoghourt, or whatever. She could be quite fearsome to strangers, I suppose; I have known few so adept at taking down a peg those whose pretensions were in excess of their performance. I think she liked to play a game of seeming ferocious, partly in sheer self-defence – as a widow for all practical purposes with Ron to bring up she had *had* to box clever – and partly for the sheer fun of the drama, just trying people out, seeing how far she could go, what they were made of, whether they would stand up to her or knuckle under. As I say, she was kindness itself, under this formidable carapace.

When I followed Neb to Fleet Street I had nowhere to live. I put up at the Strand Palace and the Regent Palace hotels, for a few nights, expecting in our naïve provincial way to find a flat toute suite. But since I was slaving away all day at the *Express* I didn't seem to find the time for house hunting, and the hotels were ruining me, so Neb invited me along to stay with him and

ma at their house in Upminster. She was just like another mother,
I couldn't have been happier; she introduced me to a breakfast
of bacon, eggs, tomatoes, fried bread and fried potatoes left over
from dinner the night before. O the digestions we used to have!

Eventually I found a flat in Maida Vale, the prostitutes'
quarter, not that I was influenced by that fact or even aware
of it, until it was too late. Later on the Neibours and the Wiggins
both took rented houses in Bromley, Kent, where we lived happily,
believe it or not, through the summer of 1940 and the autumn
blitz, in and out of one another's houses like puppies.

'Ma' mothered Kay, too, in fact she had no compunction in
telling me straight that I was by no means worthy of such a
wife, a fact of which I was well aware. We shared a lot of blitz
experiences, with which I will not bore you: Bromley was on
the Nazi milk run, one of the direct routes in to London, and
we saw quite enough.

Neb and I used to meet at Blackfriars Station and make the
train journey in the blackout together, fortified by a few pints
of wallop. It was a rum old journey, sometimes quite exciting,
always cheerful. If we had had one more than usual, and sometimes even if we hadn't (and where would we put it, anyway?)
we enjoyed sticking our heads out of the carriage window at
stations and trying to shout the names of forthcoming stations
louder than the porter on the pitch-dark platform could. Doesn't
it sound childish? ... two grown men ... well, it *was* childish,
I'm not trying to cook the book. But there wasn't any too much
fun around, childish or otherwise, and we enjoyed making a
bit more.

I can't remember the entire rigmarole, which of course shor-
tened as we drew nearer our destination, but I'm pretty sure it
ended with Ravensbourne, Shortlands, Bromley. *Ravensbourne,
Shortlands, Bromley*, we would bellow, our beery voices putting
the porter to shame. *Shortlands, Shortlands, this is Shortlands*,
Neb used to bawl, giving the words a curious tone, borrowed
from Jack Warner who was currently doing his war-winning
cries of *Maind mai baike* and *The rawlway laines* in that morale-
boosting radio show of which I forget the name, curse me. One
night we must have been more chuffed than usual for we got
above ourselves and leaped out at Shortlands, which meant a
longish drag through the blacked-out streets with shrapnel

tinkling down all round. 'You want to take cover,' an air raid warden said censoriously. 'Who doesn't?' said Neb.

I remember (shall I ever forget?) we all spent the Christmas of 1939 together at Neb's and his ma's. The phoney war was dragging on, nobody could figure out how the future might go, it was all too depressing but we hadn't begun to go short yet and we walloped into a fairly good imitation of an old-style Christmas dinner, and listened to the radio, and sang all the old songs including Neb's favourites. *Any old iron*, Harry Champion's immortal ditty, was one of several prime Cockney favourites. Neb liked the Cockney music hall songs, and he had a taste for wildly dramatic numbers, big sweeping absurdities like *Sons of the Desert*, which could be *acted* out, with large gestures. But he also had a taste for sweet sentimental ditties, and used to sing to Kay, a big man wonderfully tender and only half in jest,

> You are my honey, honeysuckle,
> I am the bee ...

and lovely old jolly ones like *Oh Mr Porter, what shall I do?* and knees-up numbers like

> My old man
> Said follow the band
> And don't dilly-dally
> On the way ...
>
> But I dillied
> And dallied,
> Dallied,
> And dillied ...

We were fans of *Itma*, of course, and Neb loved to ring up and announce *This is Funf speaking*. He was really the incarnation of the historic Londoner, the traditional sceptical sentimentalist, on a large and generous scale. His tastes were basic, the healthy tastes of the majority of the people in a free society, not high-brow, not intellectual, but not, either, by any means servile or degraded. There was a radiant sort of robust mental health in Neb and his ma: they were citizens of no mean city, they stood up tall as unquenchable human beings who might be trampled on but couldn't be kept down.

All of this healthy background was behind Neb's work, of course, his little cartoons which said so much in so small a space. I think Churchill was the only politician Neb and Neb's ma had any time for: and that was when he rose above being a politician and became the voice of a people who wouldn't be put down. We heard his great speeches together, the speeches which time will never make small or stale, the speeches which were really his chief contribution to winning the war. I mean those speeches in which he blew on the embers of national character which were in danger of being trodden out or doused by small, doubting men. *We shall fight on the beaches ... We shall never surrender.* Yes, it was he who made it our 'finest hour'. And we shared that hour, Kay and I and Neb and Neb's ma and fifty million more.

The time came when we had to part: war parted us as it parted so many. Nothing else would have parted us. We were friends for life, we are friends still. This great big shambling gentle bear of a man, with a child's open heart, a loving nature allied to a piercing wit – the rarest combination – he soldiered on in one place, and we soldiered on in many other places, and when it was all over our paths had diverged too far to be pulled together again.

Neb married a sweet girl from Barry whom we met at ma's house in Bromley, a girl who might have been Kay's sister, and now he and Babe live, as I say, in Malaga. They went there for the sunshine and the vino: Neb has bronchial trouble and Babe has arthritis. We are always hoping they'll come back home. I can't imagine a more joyous reunion than that would be. I never knew anyone so easy to get on with, so jolly and so open-hearted; so perspicacious yet so tolerant, so gentle yet so brave. There's a rare combination of qualities in dear old Neb. 'Sam, me old cocky!' he used to say when we met. I want to hear him say it again, I want to hear that voice.

As this book was going to press the sad news came that Neb had died.

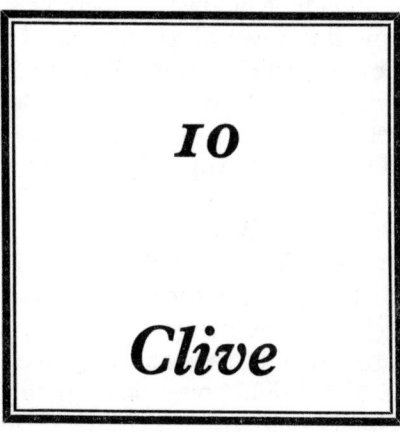

10

Clive

I WONDER how we came to know Clive? It must have had something to do with the Repertory Theatre, in Birmingham. We attended every first night there – every alternate Saturday, it was. A funny time for a first night, but that's how they arranged it, in our time, at the Rep. A new play every other Saturday. We attended in style. I got into my dinner jacket – warming in front of the fire – and Kay got into her glad rags, and off we went, the young dramatic critic and his pretty young wife, in the old Austin Seven, toddling in from our semi- in the suburbs to the liveliest theatre in the provinces. Then after the performance, drinks upstairs in the Green Room, with the actors and writers and management. And on Sunday morning, a thousand words or so to write about the play, and its performance, for first-thing-Monday-morning in the *Evening Despatch*. I allowed myself plenty of space. If the features editor couldn't allow himself plenty of space, who could?

I used to read James Agate first in *The Sunday Times* to get myself into the mood, and then walk up and down in front of the fire, dictating my piece to dear Kay, who wrote it all out meticulously in her small, round hand. What luxury! What fluency! Nowadays I couldn't dictate a telegram. I need notice to write my own name.

I think it's probably a bad thing for young critics to read old critics, but how can you stop them? I was a very fair *pasticheur* in those days, and sometimes it depended on whom I'd read last, what sounds I made. Not always: there was a core of native Wiggin, which showed through when unimpeded by better writers. But I was prone to pastiche; sometimes to parody. I could imitate Chesterton, Belloc, Agate, and a few more, quite beautifully. It arose from admiration, you see, not from dislike; from modesty, not pride. *Now* I can only parody writers whom I dislike....

Yes, I remember now, Clive had some sort of tenuous and probably unofficial job, if you could call it a job, backstage at the Rep. Not exactly assistant stage manager, not really assistant designer, not precisely scene painter, not really so humdrum as scene shifter or so tangible as scene carpenter. By no means electrician's mate. Not, I think, prompter – though that's an idea. And not actor, either, apart from a couple of walking-on parts; though that is what he was, a wonderful actor, a man playing Clive Selborne and playing it to perfection.

It isn't really surprising that after all these years, about thirty-five, we should find it a little difficult to pinpoint exactly what Clive's job was at the Rep., or with the Rep. He was always doing something slightly mysterious and indefinable, or doing nothing even more indefinably. But he was always playing Clive, and of all the roles I ever saw, and I saw thousands, there was no role I enjoyed more than Clive playing Clive. In this epoch of today he would surely be a television personality in his own right, beloved by all. Clive was out of his epoch. A little too early or a great deal too late.

Do I need to spell it out that we loved Clive and enjoyed him? We loved his performance and the actor who played it. Only the script had us foxed, at times.

Neither of us remembers clearly just how Clive came to make our acquaintance, but the same must be true of hundreds of people who knew him, and thought they knew him well. One minute you'd never heard of Clive, next minute he was a bosom friend or at least a boon companion. To Clive there was no such thing as a stranger. All people were potential friends that just didn't happen to have been switched on, yet. Like electric lights, just waiting to be switched on. He insinuated himself into your acquaintance, and your affections, like a pickpocket's hand sliding into a pocket. What an unfortunate metaphor.

At any rate, there we were, at one moment leading just ordinary old lives, next moment enriched by having the friendship of Clive. He had this gift. He could charm the scales off a pike.

What Clive was doing in Birmingham I cannot say, and could not have said at the time. His mother lived in a hydro at Harrogate, mainly, and in other hydros at other times, and Clive visited her in between jobs; and although he may well have loved her dearly I fancy he went slightly in awe of her, as he went in awe of no one else. He had irresistible charm and gaiety of manner, he had beautiful style and grace, he got on immediately with anyone he chose to get on with. The only things he didn't have were the money to go with his style and the jobs to make the money.

I remember now he was once in work selling bolts of cloth for Tootal, or someone like that. Why didn't he make a mint as a silk salesman? I can't imagine anyone better suited to the job. He had perfect taste and a natural enthusiasm for nice things, overwhelming *savoir faire*, and this grace and charm I have spoken of. He should have been a superlative salesman of fine things – or a good career diplomat. But he never was. In some way that mystified me then and mystifies me now, Clive never managed to sell himself, which is what a salesman really has to sell, the commodity he is really putting across. Well, he did sell himself, of course he did, but never in the big jackpot way that wouldn't have greatly surprised anyone who knew him. His life was lived in fits and starts of prosperity and adversity, or rather of sufficiency and insufficiency, that's nearer the mark. But you'd never know to look at him which phase he was going through at any given moment. He always looked elegant, prosperous and at ease.

Clive came and went. He would be out of our lives, the fondly remembered stuff of anecdote, for months on end, then suddenly without warning he would be very much in our lives again, bubbling over with marvellous stories. He was the best value imaginable, as entertainment, the gayest and most risible companion you could wish. If there was a certain basic sadness

beneath the gaiety, as I sometimes suspected, he kept it down
there.

Clive was born in Russia, in 1911 I think, of a Russian father
and an English mother. He and his mother escaped from Russia
after the Revolution, when he was a child of about seven. In
some mysterious way his father had him educated on the Continent – not, presumably, in Russia – until he was grown up,
then suggested that he go and live with his mother in England.
It's all very misty, but I think that is the gist of it. He didn't
actually live with her, except between jobs, but neither did he
actually live anywhere else or with anyone else in particular.
He seemed to have the entrée to a number of homes. He was a
bird of passage.

I suppose he did look slightly foreign. He was of medium
height, nicely proportioned, with a face that tapered from a
beautiful broad brow. His hair was wavy, light brown, possibly
the sort that thins out early on. He had instantly attractive,
large, gentle eyes, a mobile mouth, finely tapered long fingers.
And he dressed exquisitely. Whatever the state of his finances,
and sometimes it was not a healthy state, he looked in the money.
He took great care of his clothes. He had a lovely navy blue
Melton overcoat which, like the rest of his clothes, was made
in London by one of the top tailors, and wasn't yet paid for.
Clive was forthcoming about such things. He had a scheme to
deal with such embarrassments: its effrontery astonished us.
In spring he sent his coat back to the tailor to be checked over,
spruced up: in autumn he hoped to be in a position to pay
something off the account and get it back again in time for the
cold weather. I never knew him without it when the cold
weather came.

Financial adversity makes some of us curl up and shrivel,
die the little death. Clive did not allow it to impair his style. I
imagine he had no share of the nonconformist conscience which
has ruined the lives of some of us. Whereas people like me cannot bear to be in debt, really cannot bear it and order our whole
lives to fit our finances, 'cutting our coat according to the cloth',
people like Clive take what I have come to think is a much
healthier view, a loftier and perhaps a more cynical view. To the
Clives of this world, the style comes first – the style that suits
them must be maintained, the style which makes them happy and

fulfilled has priority over the means. It is us nonconformist nigglers who get the ulcers, worrying about paying our way, even when we *are* paying our way. There's a certain realism in the wear-now-pay-later view of our Clives – and also a certain sort of practical idealism, a touch of the doctrine of 'take no thought for the morrow', 'consider the lilies in the field', which is the very last thought we backbone-of-the-country, cash-on-the-nail wallahs ever think. Of course it's not a bit of good trying to change your nature or your natural style. It was partly because Clive's style and nature were so very different from ours that we found his company enchanting, no doubt.

Clive turned up when he turned up. In the later stages of our acquaintance, in the year or two before the 1939 war, he had a job which in a way suited him very well. He became a courier – possibly for Cook's, though I doubt it, but certainly a foreign travel courier. This was long before the entire population began to take holidays abroad, needless to say. It was a very exotic job at the time. Since Clive spoke seven languages and knew Europe like his back yard, he was for once well cast in the role, though one could not help but think he ought to have been the potentate being courier'd, not the courier. I remember he spent a lot of time in Kandersteg. He would turn up out of the blue, sometimes at breakfast, sometimes in the middle of the night, at our little rented house in Quinton, bringing with him that exotic whiff of foreign capitals and strange ways of life, utterly at ease in our rather drab little milieu and full of jokes about the customers. He rallied us.

He was a relentless mimic with a slightly childish sense of fun which flared like magnesium against the relentlessly plain background of the Midlands. Often he would take Kay out, to morning chocolate or *café creme* or afternoon tea in Fuller's café in Broad Street, near the old Prince of Wales Theatre. He made it feel like Sacher's in Vienna. Probably because he knew it would put decorous little Kay in a tizzy, he delighted to pretend he couldn't understand English, or couldn't understand English money (now the English themselves can't understand it, of course, but this was long ago, when a foreign accent in Birmingham was an interesting rarity, not a nagging reminder of irreversible change). Several times he introduced Kay to people as his wife, a situation which he could carry off with perfect aplomb for an hour on end, inventively producing a host of confirmatory details out of his childlike imagination. It could be a bit of a strain, but at least it was never dull.

We went to London and lost touch with Clive, though we never forgot him, or the holiday we had spent together at a farm at Oddingley near Droitwich, where he was known. Then just before Dunkirk, or rather just before Hitler made his great throw in the West, in the spring of 1940, I went to France as a relief war correspondent for a week or two. I was sitting down to dinner the first night in the Hotel du Commerce at Arras, which was by way of being a sort of unofficial mess for all sorts of noncombatant hangers-on, when in walked Clive in the uniform of a British officer. It was so exactly right, so precisely Clive. Only he, I felt, could have stage-managed our reunion with such perfect dramatic timing and aplomb – that word again, the word keeps coming up.

We had an entertaining week or so together, before the balloon went up. Clive was in Intelligence. We dined together every night, and talked the last hours of the phoney war away together. I could not have wished for better company in those last hours of the ticking clock.

It was during one of those sessions that Clive told me the story of his father's fur coat. His father remains to me a figure of impenetrable mystery, but apparently he had escaped to Finland and died there, leaving his fortune to Clive. The 'fortune' is the biggest and most impenetrable mystery in the entire story. Clive got permission, as only he could, to go to Finland to collect, but by that time the Russians had invaded Finland (in late 1939). The crux of the story is that all Clive found to collect was a massive and overwhelming fur coat, a coat so heavy that he had to be helped into it and helped along when he had got it on. But I gather he got it back to England; his fortune, and, one sometimes thought, an appropriate one.

I last dined with Clive on the night of 9th May, 1940. Next morning we were awakened by anti-aircraft fire at 4 a.m. My batman came in to tell me that Hitler had invaded Belgium and Holland. The phoney war was over. I never saw Clive again, never heard from him or of him. I can only draw the saddest conclusion.

I look at the telephone and think I would give a limb to hear it ring and hear again that caressing voice with a lilt and a joke in it, saying, 'Hell-*oh*, Maur-*eece*!' I need Clive. We all need a Clive.

We were different, we 'saw through' one another, we had different life-styles and different values and standards. Standards! What are they? What am I being so stuffy about? Clive was kinder than me, more generous and forthcoming and ten times as entertaining. Maybe he wasn't 'hung up', as they say nowadays, with my fixations about debt and deadlines and that sort of responsibility, maybe he was in the nicest way a little bit of a fixer and even, if we are going to talk turkey, a little tiny bit of a parasite, at times. What of it? He may not have had the benefit of the nonconformist conscience, he may not have been interested in general ideas or the state of the world, but he repaid a bit of hospitality with the gayest, most amusing talk. And it was more than just talk. It was the welling-up and flowing-over of an indomitable spirit, expressed not in barren ideology but in the grace of humour, fancy and style. If anyone was entitled to feel insecure and rootless it was dear Clive, a child of Europe, without an anchor, adrift on the sea of change. But he showed not a trace of self-pity. He had the courage to live with panache, elegant and always amusing, a benefactor of the society in which he scratched a living. He had the guts to put the end before the means.

Designing Males

I WAS Literary Editor of the London *Daily Express* when the war began. Or, at any rate, that is how I signed my business letters. The Editor, Arthur Christiansen, the legendary Chris, said that I was his Literary Editor and should so sign myself. I was nothing loth. It is a splendid title, the only title I ever coveted, except of course Undefeated Heavyweight Champion of the World, Holder of the 500 c.c. Lap Record for the Isle of Man, Footballer of the Year, or Britain's Best-Dressed Millionaire. So I was pleased, indeed a little thrilled, when Chris appointed me Literary Editor of the *Daily Express*. I went on doing exactly what I had been doing for some little while, but there was a difference inside me.

However, I must confess that the connection between my activities on that remarkable newspaper, and literature, was tenuous. It is true that I received James Agate's book reviews, and sub-edited them, thereby earning his displeasure on more than one occasion. Like all writers, he very much disliked having his copy touched by human hand, and still more by inhuman hand. Should you be so callous or cheeky as to cut one word, adjust one comma, you earned the reputation of inhumanity.

But this was wartime. Papers were drastically reduced in size, not a moment too soon if truth be told, and we were in the process of discovering the considerable professional satisfaction of filling a pint pot with a pint precisely, of real beer, instead of with half a pint of beer topped up with half a pint of froth. There is no doubt in my mind that the craft of journalism benefited from the enforced compression of those lean years. Of course we lost something, definitely, but papers had been flatulent and gassy, inflated by windy display. As they have become again today, to some extent. When we had to get down to our flimsy-feeling eight-pagers, and finally four-pagers, and cram everything in that really had to go in, we learned a lot. It wasn't as if we were cutting out miles of golden prose which screamed to be published; mainly, we were learning to economise on display, to write succinctly, and to select severely.

Of course no contributor enjoyed this process, and, as I said, Mr Agate complained to Chris more than once, in quite bitter terms, about young Wiggin's ruthlessness. But though Chris handed on to me the substance of the complaints, as in duty bound, I did not get the impression that his heart was wholly in it, and soldiered on.

This, as I have hinted, was virtually the only sector of my activities which came near to justifying the title of Literary Editor. I did not even select the books which Mr Agate should review. Publishers sent them to him direct; a practice which annoys Literary Editors intensely, and with reason. He was very much the Great Panjandrum, was Agate, very egotistical and self-centred. I disliked him and it was mutual. He was a bit of a bully, I thought. Though I met him only a couple of times, in the office, and had only a few acrimonious telephone conversations with him, I was satisfied that a man who could treat a fellow human being as he treated me, i.e. like dirt, was not a very nice sort of person. Of course he was brilliant, highly gifted: I'm sure he was worth every penny they paid him. Personally I had some reservations about a man who used his gifts and opportunities to make writers and actors and junior persons feel small. He must have enjoyed humiliating people or he wouldn't have done it so often. I suppose I wouldn't have minded if he had used his gift to deflate the pompous hypocrites and windbags who were running things, the ghastly Establishment, who steered us from one disaster to the next. But he didn't. He kept on the right side of that sort, he was a fully-paid-up member of the Establishment even if only as a sort of licensed court jester. He knew which side his bread was buttered on. He actually admired success. But he would reduce a struggling actress to tears by a sentence which could well have been omitted, he would 'review' a novel that was not worth reviewing and should not have been mentioned, simply to show off his considerable talent for ridicule. I don't judge his judgement: it was very acute. I merely say that he was overbearing to very minor helpless figures who could only suffer and not hit back.

I don't know how it was at *The Sunday Times*, where he was drama critic, but at the *Daily Express* he was treated with great respect and even subservience. He had established himself as a Somebody, a figure, a celebrity. He was one of those critics who use London as his personal stage, fond of the spotlight, acting out a role. This went down well with Lord Beaverbrook, and, no doubt, with Lord Kemsley, and of course the underlings took their line from the top, and laid out the carpet for him.

He was indisputably one of the great critics, essayists and diarists of his day, marvellously readable, sound and acute. I read the bulk of his work with joy. But those end paragraphs, so waspish and wounding, and unnecessary.... I found it hard to forgive him those. And when he came the old acid with me personally, laying down the law *de haut en bas* as if I were some sort of footman or lackey, I responded as I have always responded to haughty snootiness from life's Somebodies: I changed instantly from the mildest, most easy-going soft ha'porth on the domestic scene into a spitting, scratching and clawing jungle creature.

One of the several faults which have kept me from reaching the top in my profession is my inability to take 'top people' as seriously as they take themselves. I can't take them seriously at all. This has been my most serious handicap. My values must be very perverse; they are certainly topsy-turvy. I don't claim to be right: I am just recording facts as observed by a professional observer who has two eyes and ears the same as most people and virtually no preconceptions about how to use them. With a few golden exceptions, which I am happy to celebrate, I have found top people slightly disappointing. There is perhaps only one sense in which I might be said to have a Christian element in my make-up, and that is that I heartily concur in, I enthusiastically support, the wistful notion that it is probably a good deal easier for a camel to skip lightly through the eye of a needle than for a rich man to get into heaven. I simply cannot see how a man can become rich, or powerful, unless he is defective in the human qualities which I happen to admire and enjoy. If I had my time again I think I'd have a go at being Robin Hood, an admirable invention of that spontaneous mythology which reminds us, time and again, that you can't fool all the people all of the time.

If I wasn't really a literary editor, what was I? I was features editor again, but a minor or subsidiary one, the real features editor being a most remarkable person named John Rayner, whom we called our Day Assistant Editor. There were three great features editors in my generation: John Rayner, Harold Keeble, and Hugh Cudlipp. I never met Mr Cudlipp, who was with the *Mirror* and *Pictorial* outfit, and who turned out to be by far the most durable and influential of the three. I never even worked with Mr Keeble, who moved on from the *Express* to the *Mail*, but I knew him fairly well and whole-heartedly admired his brilliance, especially as a typographer and layout designer, while being amused by his uncritical acceptance of the vulgar-naïve Beaverbrook-Christiansen criteria of what was interesting and admirable in this crazy world. But I worked alongside Mr Rayner and count that one of the privileges of my life.

John Rayner was so brilliant that it has always been a mystery to me that he never became one of the greatest figures in the publishing world. But perhaps I simply didn't know him well enough? He was reserved and unforthcoming in a personal sense and I never penetrated that rather aloof, even forbidding, façade. He could be icy. With me he was invariably a kindly taskmaster, a painstaking teacher; when I went wrong, he pointed out the error of my ways gently, courteously, teaching me while reproving me. He taught me almost everything I ever learned about typography and layout – he was teaching me remotely, without knowing it, long before we met. For it was his pages in the *Daily Express* which fascinated me while I was struggling to learn my way around in Birmingham, and my pages in the *Despatch* which led him to offer me a job. I think he recognised that I was not a mere copyist, but a pilgrim with the same approach, the same ideals; a visualiser who shared his philosophy of design and display.

The design of newspapers is organic or it is nothing. Mr Rayner invented the *Express* style and brought it to its zenith of perfection. It was a style which I found completely congenial; logical and harmonious, exciting and beautiful. It has now vanished from the face of the earth, but in its heyday it set standards, both aesthetic and logical, if they aren't the same thing, which had never been approached before and have not been surpassed since.

I lost the chance of a commission by arguing this case before a Selection Board at the Air Ministry. One of the languid snooty examiners asked me with a barely-concealed sneer how I could justify having worked on the *Daily Express* – instead of something like the *Manchester Guardian* or *The Times* or *Telegraph*. I told him. I gave him the full treatment. I sold my possibly naïve notion of the holy beauty of the *Daily Express* with more fervour than I might have used had I not detected the sneer. In fact I did not think very much of the *Daily Express* as a communicator, its politics left me cold and I never shared its assumptions about the readers and their limitations – summed up in Strube's 'Little Man', which always seemed to me an absurd, offensive and condescending image.

George Strube was another of the leading communicators with whom I clashed during my time as Literary Editor. If I so much as put a postage-stamp-size half-tone block within a foot of his cartoon, on the Leader Page, he was running to the Editor complaining that I was deliberately distracting attention away from his great big drawing. I wasn't trying to do anything of the kind but, when confronted, naturally I defended the unpopular proposition that if a great big cartoon couldn't stand the competition of a tiny little half-tone shot way down the page, there must be something wrong with the cartoon. That went down very badly. But I've found that vanity is by no means confined to the failures among us. Some of the most successful are among the most touchy.

But if I didn't have the authentic *Express*-think running in my veins, at any rate I had no doubts whatever about the superiority of the *Express* visual style, its style of presentation and projection. Within the natural limitations of his socio-political stance, which was to my mind rather naïve, Arthur Christiansen was a really great editor, a technical editor who liberated some remarkable technicians to do their best work for him. These included not only Rayner and Keeble, but such as Bill Knott, dear old Knotto, the chief sub-editor, who sometimes made his news pages absolute little works of art, full of fun and visual drama and interest; and Bertie Gunn, Chris's deputy, who also had a flair for this business, and of whom I shall have to write later when I come to his days as Editor of the *Evening Standard*.

So I gave it to this Air Force mandarin, hot and strong, and for full measure allowed it to be understood that I found his attitude disgustingly reactionary and undemocratic. Not that I was democracy's leading defender in the ordinary way, I was in fact politically a bit lax and sceptical, if not actually cynical, and had seen too much of human nature including my own to cherish any very strong convictions that government by the people was really likely to be more effective than government by the bastards who kept them down. Though of course in the last analysis if you're human at all you must fight against autocracy and tyranny. I wasn't so libertarian and democratic as all that or I wouldn't have been there at Air Ministry bumming for a commission to get me out of the dreary old ranks, would I?

This plum with the rings on his sleeves went rather red and cut me off pretty short, remarking that he hadn't asked me for a sales spiel. I said I thought that was precisely what he had asked me for. I was dismissed and although they said they'd 'let me know' I knew I'd missed the boat again. Ah well. 'And they came nigh unto barathea. . . .' No smooth barathea uniform for yours t. Back to the itchy Air Force issue trousers, and weren't they just?

When I say that John Rayner 'invented' the *Express* style I am laying myself open to correction. Perhaps Chris himself invented it. But without doubt it was Rayner who, with Keeble as his enthusiastic and brilliant adjutant, brought the typography and the visual philosophy of the paper, especially its many feature pages, to that peak-level of logic, harmony, polish and high drama which they attained in the mid and late 'Thirties. Many were the copyists, but the copies could never be mistaken for the original – if only because the driving force behind the *Express* look was a coherent philosophy of the aesthetics of design. It is difficult to counterfeit a truly organic approach in which the look of the thing cannot be separated from the meaning of the thing. 'The surface of things *is* the heart of things,' said one of the Powys brothers; and this lesson had been absorbed by Chris, Rayner, Keeble, Gunn and Knotto. In varying degrees, of course. Very. In John Rayner's case, it was a matter of total integration – medium and message became one, it was not just a question of 'taste' (though his taste was austere and exquisite, virtually infallible) but a question of logic. Everything from the tint of the paper, the newsprint – an important factor – through the selection of type faces and rules, drop letters and face-measures, right down to the infinitely calculated stylisation of by-lines and captions.... Every detail was part of the coherent philosophy, in which harmony grew out of order, beauty out of discipline, drama out of restraint.

I absorbed all this so completely that to this day I can reproduce on the layout bench a dozen, a score of Rayner's and Keeble's pages, down almost to the last detail, just as they were drawn thirty or forty years ago.

John Rayner was a tremendously impressive figure, tall, very handsome, aristocratic in demeanour. He looked very like a blond version of Douglas Bader. He wore beautiful clothes, but with a certain careless air; he sometimes kept his trousers up with a belt or tie. He was educated at Westminster School and, on the day on which I joined the *Daily Express*, he spent his lunch time in getting married to a daughter of Sir Bolton Eyres-Monsell, a politician who became a peer. I had no inkling of this until I saw his picture, and of course his bride's, in an afternoon edition of the London *Evening News*. He never mentioned it. I thought what a wonderfully casual, aristocratic way of going about it. He came back a trifle happy, accompanied by Tom Driberg if memory serves, the pioneer who was writing the William Hickey column which he founded and made famous and which was never anything near so good after he gave it up. Again, a question of organic style: you can't really imitate a style just by copying mannerisms: it degenerates into pastiche. Mr Rayner always lunched 'up West', and came back smoking a cigar. It's commonplace now, of course, but in those days it was quite exceptional. Some resented the Rayner manner, needless to say; I suppose I might easily have done so myself, it was so unlike what I was used to and therefore believed right and proper. But he was never snooty with me; on the contrary, he made me feel good, above myself.

He lived in a corner office, the best office on the editorial floor, overlooking Fleet Street. I inherited it from him for some months when he fell ill. It was partitioned off by opaque glass, but not right to the ceiling. Rayner's manner of summoning his underlings was quite distinctive. He simply shouted their names, and they trotted in – a touch of the old public school fag system, I imagine. *'Baerlein!'* he would call, in that piercing withering voice; and dear Tony Baerlein, an Old Etonian who joined the R.A.F. and was killed on his first operational flight, would drop whatever he was struggling with and trot in. Really just like fag and fag master. This authoritarian manner wouldn't have suited me at all, my career on the *Express* would have ended on Day One. But for some reason, and I put it down to an innate delicacy of feeling, Rayner never tried it on me. I dare say he could see that I wasn't public school material and would be upset by an approach which the Old Etonian took as perfectly natural. At any rate, if he wanted me he either sent his secretary, the redoubtable Miss Chaundy, to fetch me from the outer darkness of the big open-plan office, or sauntered out himself. And, as I have said, invariably treated me as a rational co-worker.

I've often asked myself why it was that I felt such unspoiled affection and admiration for this Olympian figure, for he epitomised certain qualities (of manner, personal style) to which in lesser men I was often quite allergic. I conclude that it was partly because he treated me as a fellow pilgrim following the same star (which was true, professionally speaking) and partly because I saw in him, *as a worker*, not necessarily as a person but as a creative professional, the ultimate distillation of precisely those qualities which I most admired and which I would have liked to find in myself.

However that may be, it is John Rayner whom I remember with something absurdly approaching reverence, as the key figure in the formation of my newspaper philosophy. I know my limitations. Ideally, I should have remained his side-kick. Had he become an Editor, I might have made a good and happy features editor working to him, as I was, without doubt, when working to Ben, though Ben was not a Rayner. But life is never ideal. The

war started quite soon after I went to work on the *Express.*
Rayner went away to work for the Political Intelligence Department of the Foreign Office, and ended up working there under
Harold Keeble; the positions reversed. They tried to get me out
of the R.A.F. to work with them, but the R.A.F. in its wisdom
declined to let me go. After the war it was Keeble who returned
to Fleet Street. Rayner I lost sight of, for some years, though
I know that he went into the world of book production. Until very
recently, I mourned him as the Editor I most needed to work
for, and never did. Actually I did badly on the *Express,* failed
to live up to the promise of Birmingham, on the strength of
which John Rayner had recruited me. I made a mess of my
chances, for various reasons that are not to my credit. I don't
wish to gloss over it. But war would have made a mess of them
anyway.

It was a delight to see Rayner lay out a page; his draughtsmanship was delicate and true, the finish exquisite. The page went
down to the printers completely ready and finished: there was
the minimum of follow-up work for the stone sub to do, though
I spent hours on the stone just the same, feeling so released and
happy there, in that special atmosphere which suited me to
perfection – a sort of factory, precise and productive, full of
activity and the special smells and light sounds of a composing
room, but with the added bonus of being concerned in the production of the word-thing, the page, *glory alleluia.* To preside
over that transformation scene, when the page that was merely
so many marks on a sheet of paper became an objective and
tangible reality, an actual page in type, in metal, encased in its
forme, ready to be proofed and moulded for the rotary presses –
this was what I liked almost best of all in the entire spectrum of
experiences concerned with newspapers.

As I said, I never actually worked with or for Harold Keeble,
but I know his style. He laid out a page more dramatically than
John Rayner, in the sense that his draughtsmanship was bolder,
freer, more vigorous and blacker. 'When I draw 72 point, it *is*
72 point,' he declared to me one day over lunch at Kettner's
in Soho. 'When I draw 48 point it *is* 48 point.' He had this
splendid certainty, like a painter's who takes his brush and
makes just one firm and sure stroke. In a sense that is not wholly
far-fetched, designing a page is like making a picture. Keeble's

pictures were above all vigorous, full of vivacity. Whether he quite had the refined sensibilities of John Rayner, or the typographical scholarship, I'm in some doubt.

On the one hand, when he turned to tabloid design, in his days on the *Mirror*, he achieved some very striking pages, using the horrid condensed sanserif faces, the brutal gothic types, with enlightened authority, and lightening them subtly by his clever use of white space and light faces. On the other hand, his work on the *Express* after the war showed, I thought, a certain decline. The sheer power was still there, but I thought I detected a certain loss of that essential logic which is at the root of all great design. A trace of strain began to show (or so I thought, devoted as I was to the great Age of the Enlightenment presided over by Rayner). The use of news-page type faces on the feature pages depressed me; I thought I saw the refinement being blurred. But against that, there is the evidence of his brilliant work on the *Sunday Express* during the early years of war, when he was in fact the working editor under the controlling direction of John Gordon. He revolutionised the look of that paper almost overnight, and the news pages have never looked so fine. He was a very versatile and restless perfectionist, Harold Keeble, and would never leave a page alone, improving it in detail all the way along, until sometimes the hour grew late and the printer restive. Whereas when Rayner sent his layout down, he had finished.

Keeble was a north country lad, like Don Iddon. I'm not sure if they came from the same town, but certainly they were boyhood friends, and I first met Keeble at the Birmingham office, when he had called in to see Don, swirling to the kerb, to our amazement, in his open or convertible Hudson Terraplane, an opulent American car, and wearing his camel hair coat which was then almost the uniform of success on the *Express*. Keeble had got there first, he was ahead of us; Don couldn't wait to get down there to join him, and in my time I followed them. Not that I ever wholly shared their raptures over the Big Smoke: I always had reservations about the quality of life in that city. But Harold, like Don, accepted it as *the* goal, the great city where life was infinitely more exciting and rewarding and somehow *real*. I have to confess that while I was in his company I was persuaded that it really did have glamour, for Harold exuded glamour, he was a truly glamorous young man.

Apart from his brilliance as a designer, he was a perfect *Express* features editor in the sense that he really was ravished by the kaleidoscopic surface of metropolitan life, he really enjoyed being up-to-date or preferably a step ahead, he was expansive and gregarious in a strictly limited, useful way – he liked to frequent fashionable restaurants, hobnob with leading figures, top models, celebrities, power-game figures, men and women on the make. He was ideally cast by temperament and talent to be a leading denizen of the black glasshouse – and with it all, let me make this clear, he was entertaining company, gay and resourceful and thoroughly enjoying the tower of Babel.

I was never so happy in Fleet Street as I had been in the provinces, and one good reason was that I realised with perfect clarity that, nippy as I was, I was definitely inferior as a craftsman to at least two of my own kind, Harold Keeble and John Rayner. I could just about keep up with them, at my best, but I realised that they were teaching me, I wasn't teaching them. I was not the first to discover that they play it faster, and rougher, in Division One than in Division Two.

With the great Chris himself, Arthur Christiansen, I enjoyed a happy but perhaps a fundamentally unsatisfactory relationship. Yes, it can be both things. I was happy because he was such a good father figure to me, always indulgent even when exasperated by my reluctance to take seriously what he thought serious. This was the great difference between Keeble and myself. Harold told me that Chris's company stimulated him, made him sparkle, live above himself. On me, Chris had the opposite effect. He exuded such a superabundance of vitality and drive that I felt enervated in his presence. He had quite enough energy for both of us, and though I quite enjoyed seeing him exude it, I didn't feel called upon to supplement it. Chris gave me the impression that he could produce the paper quite competently single-handed, and I didn't feel I should deprive him of the pleasure.

I have been told that he grew a little arrogant with success. If so, he had cause. He hoisted the circulation of the *Daily Express* to undreamed-of-figures, and he did it by producing a clean paper, never a hint of salacity, which persuaded its readers that life was vivid and sparkling when it was in fact quite otherwise, for most people. Like the Lancashire lads, Iddon and Keeble, but in superabundant measure, Chris, the boy from Wallasey on Merseyside, brought to Fleet Street this naïvely joyous and uncritical and in the last analysis profoundly provincial acceptance of the London life-style, the metropolitan glamour; they transferred their joy in it to their sparkling pages and persuaded a great many readers that life was as exciting as *they* found it. They were very much men of their time.

12

The Mask of War

Taffy

I WENT to war from Bloxwich station, via Blackpool. As the train crawled northwards through the melancholy ravaged landscape of late October, as the Black Country merged into the pastoral country of Cheshire and again into the industrial wilderness of Lancashire, other recruits got in, all immediately recognisable by their hopelessness. We were a miserable bunch which disembarked at Blackpool. Memories of pre-war high jinks on the Golden Mile and South Beach Funfair gruelled the irony of the situation into us like grit ground in under an iron heel.

At Blackpool we were seized, affronted and corralled, on the station itself, by a small bunch of regular NCOs like terriers, who sorted us into packs and proceeded to march us through the wintry streets, endlessly, at high speed, bound for our digs, into which we were decanted by squads, like sacks of coal or crates of small, cheap pets. For our first month in the R.A.F. we were to live in those digs, drilling every day on the prom, in side streets, on the football pitch, at the baths. Basic training turned us from civilians into airmen, or so it was believed.

It was better than barracks, anyway. At least in the evening we were a family in a house, and ghastly though the food was, grim our landlord and landlady, at least we drew some shreds of comfort from this last lingering attenuated touch of civilian life. We huddled together in our little drab temporary home like brothers. We were paid two shillings a day of which one shilling was allocated to our wives. Out of the seven shillings remaining to us we bought our blanco and Brasso and boot polish, an occasional fish and chip supper and fortnightly pint of beer, and we still were naïve enough to squander a bob or two on pathetic little group photographs, some of which still exist, fading now, showing us wearing our new uniforms very badly, our side caps perched at weird angles on shorn heads, but our brasses blinking bravely.

From Blackpool we went to St Athan in darkest Glamorgan, a huge permanent Royal Air Force station where we did our technical training. That was the worst, the blackest winter of my life. I nearly died of boredom. I was to find myself able to face danger, later in the war, with tolerable equanimity, but the sheer boredom of technical training so enervated my spirit that I really became another person. I really think my sanity was saved by the charming, cynical company of Maurice Cooper, an aristocratic displaced person who cheered me up by being even more sceptical than I was. Where are you now, Maurice dear? I hope that your pessimism was misplaced. Bless you for all you were.

One was neither at war nor at peace, neither a soldier nor a civilian; but a nondescript anonymous being, barely human, who was required to show interest – and a lively interest, or else – in the ineffably dreary business of taking aeroplanes to pieces and putting them together again. I had only joined the Air Force in pique, having been (wisely) turned down by the Brigade of Guards on physical grounds and not wishing to join any military unit other than the Guards. My sight, if nothing else, kept me out of flying duties, and there seemed nothing else for it but to join the ground forces of the R.A.F. Later on, when I joined a Repair and Salvage unit of the Second Tactical Air Force in preparation for the Normandy campaign, and later still when I served with the Servicing Commando of 2nd TAF, I found life wondrously more interesting. But first there were two or three years of utter boredom to be got through. I volunteered at every opportunity, sought transfer to everything going – the R.A.F. Regiment, aircrew duties as a Flight Engineer, the tank corps, the Political Intelligence Department of the Foreign Office (which actually *sought* my services). But it was no go. Some ninety pounds sterling had been spent on making me an aircraft fitter, and they weren't going to waste it. So I soldiered on.

Three factors saved my precarious sanity during those boring years. First, that I took the war against Nazism seriously enough to want it won; call it a sense of duty. Second, that I greatly enjoyed the freedom from careerism which service implied. I rather liked the semi-monastic poverty of the life, with all material vulgar ambitions swept away. That appealed to the masochist in me, the part which regrets aggressiveness and competition. I liked the comradely sharing. It was not exactly an open society – the society for which I have always craved – but despite its hierarchical structure, there was still a sense of being 'a man for a' that', which appealed to something in my nature. And third, I met some interesting characters.

Group Captain Taffy Jones was in command at the dreary new station called Llandow (No. 53 Operational Training Unit), to which we were transported when our technical training at St Athan was over. He was a wild one. I presume that he was a fighter pilot of the First World War, now living it up vicariously among the Spitfire pilots who came to us for their final operational training. He was shorter than he would have liked, but stocky and strong. He wore a fierce fighter pilot moustache in black, his Welsh eyes flashed and flickered and his language was intemperate but enthralling. It was my pleasure and privilege to be present on the sempiternal morning when Taffy took up a Spitfire to show various visiting dignitaries (and the pupils) how it should be done. He yanked the undercarriage up just a fraction too soon and the aircraft skud along on its belly amid a shower of sparks and a great, great silence. We changed the propeller, undercarriage, radiator and quite a number of other items, each more boring than the last, at high speed and with some stealth, and by next morning the thing was not only as good as new, but, mysteriously, no one ever said anything about it having been impaired, let alone repaired.

I was very fond of Taffy, though in view of the social gulf between Group Captain and bleedin' erk I was not able to express my admiration very clearly. We only once came at loggerheads, and that in a curious way. We were having some sort of barmy exercise designed to sharpen up our station security, which was quite lax, and I was on sentry-go outside a dreary great hut in which many of my mates were having a quiet zizz. My orders were unequivocally clear: 'Challenge every bugger who approaches, make them prove their identity.' Naturally I took this to mean challenge every unidentified bugger. So when Taffy stalked up, bristling and quivering as usual, instead of challenging him I came to attention very smartly indeed and threw him up a salute so crisp that I bruised my fingers on the rifle I was bearing at the sli-hope. Taffy ground to a halt, fairly foaming. His Welsh voice rose to a screech and I knew it wasn't any of that there *hwyl*.

'*Why* didn't you challenge me, you blithering horrible erk, you?'

'Because you are Croup Captain Chorns, our C.O.,' I retorted, laying on the Welsh accent as thick as a double helping of Naafi beans. Not that one ever got a double helping.

This fixed him, I could see that. Wrath strove with laughter. But he wasn't going to let me get away with it.

'To you or to you not haff specific orters to challenge everypody who approaches you?'

'My specific orters are to challenge effery unidentified pugger who approaches, sir. You are not an unidentified pugger, sir.'

By this time the uproar had brought the Flight Sergeant i/c Discip. out of the hut, looking lost as usual. The Flying Officer who accompanied Taffy one pace to the rear didn't know where to look, he was enjoying himself so much, and the rather elderly major of the Coldstream Guards who was running the security exercise and who had just arrived looked as if he did not wish to believe the evidence of his senses.

'Flight Sergeant,' Taffy cried, 'I want this airman put under close arrest. He failed to challenge me. What were your specific orters to this man?'

To everyone's surprise the Flight Sergeant began to laugh. I realised in a flash that he had been at the rum ration already. Because we were on this security exercise and up all night a quantity of Navy issue rum had been brought to the hut and placed in the Flight Sergeant's charge. Obviously he had been unable to resist taking a pannikin or two.

'I told him to challenge every unidentified bugger who approached,' said the Flight Sergeant, very thick and grinning all over his homely mug.

'You're drunk, Flight Sergeant,' Taffy snapped.

'No, sir,' said Chiefy. 'Can't be. I'm standing up.'

'Fetch the bloody Coldstream,' rasped Taffy, perfectly well aware that that elegant major was standing at his elbow. 'Show him what a dog's breakfast he's made of the whole boiling.'

Officers intervened tactfully to draw Taffy away, the Flight Sergeant was quietly withdrawn, the officers argued the toss among themselves for quite a time, and I remained nominally on sentry-go at the door. As he began to walk away Taffy suddenly remembered me. He came back.

'See me in the morning,' he said sharply, looking me fiercely in the eye. 'Ten o'clock sharp.'

'Sir!'

Next morning I was duly wheeled in. It was an unorthodox situation. I wasn't under arrest, so any rollicking would be unofficial. Strange?

I threw one up and awaited the wrath to come.

'Why don't you apply for a commission?' Taffy said, affably.

I took a deep breath.

'No qualifications, sir,' I replied. 'I've tried. I'm a Group One tradesman and therefore ineligible. Except for engineering branch. And I haven't got a degree in engineering.'

'What *have* you got a degree in?'

'History, sir.'

'Aberystwyth?'

'Oxford, if you don't mind.'

'Too bloody good for Aberystwyth, is it?'

'Not good enough, sir.'

Taffy turned to the Flying Officer who invariably stood one pace to the rear at his right elbow.

'See what I mean? Crafty pugger. Just what we need to deal with all the bumf from Group. Make a good adj, eh?'

'Yes, sir.' The assistant adjutant winked at me over Taffy's head.

'I take it you can read and write, then,' said Taffy, glaring at me.

'English.'

'I thought you were Welsh?'

'Just a drop of Welsh blood, sir. I pass myself off as English.'

'You were putting it on, then, yesterday. You were taking the piss out of your commanding officer?'

'God forbid, sir. It just comes over me when I'm excited.'

Taffy wrestled with his better self for some time.

'All right,' he said. 'I'm going to put you up. I'll sign the form myself. Want them to know it isn't a ——ing F.O. recommending you, don't we?' He glared over his shoulder at the F.O.

'As you say, sir,' said the F.O., winking at me again.

It came to nothing. I ended up as a sergeant. But I've never forgotten that Taffy tried. I served under some good commanding officers, but Taffy was the liveliest personality of them all.

Matelot

Matelot, matelot, where you go my heart goes with you. He was singing quietly as if to himself, leaning over the bows of the LCT as she ploughed her way through the Solent. He was a young sailor and this was his first operational voyage.

So it was for most of us. I hoped the skipper had got a bit of operational experience but it wasn't for a mere passenger to ask. He too looked absurdly young. I made a tour of the Landing Craft Tank as we stood out from the shore, bound for Normandy, picking my way around and over the Bedford lorries, the mobile crane and the bulldozer with which she was laden. I was looking for hardened, tough-looking matelots who looked as if they might have got some practice in running aground on enemy coasts. They all looked very young to me. But they looked calm, too.

The young Ordinary Seaman in the bows had a round skull on which pale golden hair grew, a round baby-face and baby-blue eyes. I don't think he needed to shave. He was just a boy. *There'll be bluebirds over The white cliffs of Dover*, he sang, very softly. He came from County Durham.

We lay off the French coast throughout the night, wearing our tin hats. The shrapnel whistled down. Everything with a trigger seemed to be firing. The German aircraft flew over in ones and twos, dropping flares. The beachhead was livid was gunflashes and flares. We knew our chaps had got ashore well, but they hadn't got too far inland, and now the coastal strip and the offshore belt of crowded sea, a navigator's nightmare, were alike erupting in continuous gunfire.

I went up to the bows and there was the boy sailor from County Durham leaning over the side, watching the show. I gave him a fag. We automatically ducked our heads together and cupped our hands to hide the flame. The night was as bright as day, but it was a habit.

'Sooner you than me, sarge,' he said, nodding towards the shore.

'Can't say I'm all that keen myself.'

'Me for good old Gosport,' the sailor said. 'Soon as we've run you lot ashore we'll be hopping across to collect the next lot. I know where I'd sooner be.'

I wasn't too hilarious about the situation myself. The noise, the apparent confusion, the uncertainty, weighed against the unquestionable thrill of the moment, the indubitable sense of high adventure. But I felt it incumbent upon me to speak in appropriate platitudes. I was the older man, I must set an example, I was humping on my back the deadweight of thirty-two years of literature and received attitudes.... How could I fail to speak in appropriate platitudes? What would Tom Merry have said at this moment?

'Sooner we're in, sooner it'll be over,' I said. Not original, not inspiring particularly; but nice and obvious and incontrovertible.

'You're right there, sarge,' the boy said. 'The buzz is it'll all be over by Christmas.'

'Is that the buzz in the Navy?'

'Sure. They've got *Warspite* bombarding the Jerry positions just down the coast. Did you see her?'

'That should do it,' I said encouragingly. I had indeed seen her, the old lady, lazily pumping the occasional fifteen-inch shell over into the hinterland. Privately I thought it might take a bit more than one battleship to break the morale of Rommel and the Seventh Army, but doubtless every little helped. As the night wore on and the realisation that one was actually committed to that maelstrom ashore took possession of the incredulous nerve-endings, I felt myself going under to a life of platitude. Every little helps....

'Every little helps,' I heard myself say.

'*Warspite*'s not so little,' the sailor said, after a moment's pause for thought. He sounded a bit hurt.

'You fancy serving on a battle wagon?' I asked.

'Fancy serving on a *real* ship, sarge,' he said with warmth in his voice. 'This bloody thing's nobbut a tin box.'

The LCT was indeed the plainest, nay, the ugliest, the most unashamedly utilitarian, slab-sided, dead rectangular box of thin steel plate. Cheap and nasty. I could understand how a sailor might feel about her. But – here it came again – ours not to reason why. They also serve.... I felt awash in platitudes. It's the stage management, I thought helplessly. In circumstances like these, how can you feel anything but appropriate platitudes? Nothing else fitted. We exchanged a few more. Suddenly it all palled, the noise, the lights, the platitudes, the whole absurdity and adventure.

'Think I'll turn in,' I said. 'Get me head down.'

'You get your head down, sarge,' the boy answered. 'If I wasn't on watch I'd do the same myself. See you bright and early.'

Incredibly, we slept. The boy woke me at first light, with a fag and a mug of tea. He didn't have to. I rolled out from under my truck and shivered in the light thin air of dawn.

'We're going in in half an hour,' he said. 'The bosun says so.'

'The bosun knows,' I said sagely.

In a pig's eye the bosun knows. We hung around till mid-morning, start engines, stop engines, warm up, cool down. Then suddenly it was all action and bustle. The LCT swung round for the last time and drove furiously in under full power, straight at the shelving beach. The skeletons of holiday houses looked strangely intact. We drove in between wrecks towards a sailor waving flags.

I started the engine of the Bedford and engaged emergency low gear, four-wheel drive.

The boy sailor appeared at the window.

'Keep your foot down, sarge!'

'I will. Good luck.'

'So long, sarge.'

'So long.'

Down into five feet of salt water, flat out in emergency low gear, four-wheel drive, O God don't let her stall, Normandy here we come.

Matelot, matelot, where you go my heart goes with you.

An Old Lady

WE dug our slit trenches in a little orchard of cider apples. The nearest place was a hamlet called Ellon, in the bocage country of Normandy.

I saw through the hedge a little row of red-brick cottages, three or perhaps four. When we had finished work for the day we washed ourselves in petrol cans cut in half, and wandered out to talk to the people who were living through the battle, in their own homes.

We took some tea which we begged from Harry Keighley, the sergeant cook, and a few cans of soup, nothing much; we were still on K rations but Harry had a little bit of stuff put aside.

An old lady was collecting the washing which she had spread on the hedgerows. The storms of early June had died away and it was tranquil dusty weather, fine and hot.

She asked me into her cottage, the end of the row nearest to the enemy. I had to show her how to make tea. She had never drunk tea before. She didn't have a teapot, so I brewed it in a jug, with a cloth over the top to hold the steam in while it brewed. We drew the water from a well with a sandy bottom, as pure as one could wish. It was chalk stream country.

I don't think she really liked the flavour very much, but there was no coffee to be had and even tea was better than nothing. And I gave her a bit of chocolate which she liked very much indeed.

Thereafter for the few days we were stuck there I managed to see the old lady every evening, just for a few minutes, to chat and brew her a cup of tea and chop wood and chat about things. She told me that she had lost a son in the Great War. She was all alone and very old.

I reassured her about the course of the war as best I could. She was strangely philosophical about *les sales Boches*, whom she had so much reason to detest. I got the impression that the Boches had behaved quite nicely in Normandy, around those parts, while waiting for us to come and knock the place about and push them out. At any rate she bore no malice. All soldiers were a nuisance. One understood that. *Libération* was a nice big word.

We got the tip to pack up and push off at first light. It was growing dusky when I visited the old lady for the last time, to say goodbye. There was just time to chop her a bit more kindling for the stove, but she didn't want any tea. I don't think she liked it really.

She insisted that I stay and have supper with her. She drew a jug of that bitter green cider and laid two places, with saucers, and she put an artichoke on each saucer. That was the lot.

I demurred, but she insisted.

'*Pour la cérémonie,*' she said.

We broke up our artichokes and ate them with our fingers, and drank the bitter cider in ceremonious little toasts. To good health, to victory, to safe returns. I got the impression that safe returns and victories did not interest her very much, any more, but good health made sense. We drank to *la paix*.

I made a promise which I really thought I might keep, to return and see her again after *la victoire*. I was going to bring her chocolate and coffee and we would eat again together, *pour la cérémonie*. But when I went back in 1948 she was dead.

She came to the door of the cottage to see me off. The soft light of the candle was behind her and her old face was in shadow. She was really very old.

I went through the little cottage garden, a few steps only to the gate, and turned and waved. She raised her hand as in a benediction.

It was quite absurd, but I found myself closing the gate quietly.

A citizen of Beauvais

WE laagered in a meadow alongside a dense dark wood near the town of Beauvais. We pulled the trucks into three sides of a square and formed up loosely within the open square while the C.O. made a speech. He had got the wire from on high that we were to be taken out of the war for a few days. Supplies were running short and we were not sufficiently important or valorous to get a share of them. It had been a long, fast dash across France after the Normandy battle ended in breakthrough, and the army was pressing on into Belgium and even towards Holland. But everything was still coming in over the beach-head, the Mulberry harbour at Arromanches, hundreds of miles behind the leading units. We were running short of everything and until the army and navy got Antwerp opened again we were likely to stay short. So it was first things first and for us that meant no petrol, precious little food, and a nice rest. Post your sentries – there might still be bands of stragglers skulking in the woods – and get stuck in to servicing your equipment.

With which the C.O. started his jeep and, accompanied by every officer who could squeeze in or hang on, departed for Paris, newly liberated and everybody's dream city.

The rations for those who stayed behind were four hard biscuits and two slices of bully a day.

Needless to say, the competition for a place in the C.O.'s little caravan of hedonists was very keen. It drew forth several instructive examples of grovelling servility, guile and disingenuousness. Possibly I am defective in the libido, though I'd hardly have thought so; there are those who would find the suggestion risible; at any rate I actually welcomed the opportunity for a couple of days rest and quiet, and, though very fond of Paris, dream city that it is, I felt that the pressure of liberators might well show La Ville Lumière in one of its less attractive lights. As, indeed, from all accounts, it did.

But that was certainly a minority view, and the good wishes which followed the C.O.'s party out of the field would surely have touched their hearts, could they have heard them. Vivid and ingenious were the imaginative descriptions of the sexual adventures which some dreamers supposed to lie in wait for that gallant party. Several expressed the fervent hope that venereal disease in all its forms would be among their rewards.

My comrades in arms expressed themselves in the bitter monotonous language of the barrack room, a stunted usage which was har dto bear, even though one soon took to it oneself in sheer self-defence (it was, after all, the language to be learned, if communication were to be established at all). I have never quite shaken off the damaging effects on my speech of five-and-a-half years of barrack room language.

Perhaps the angriest of my abandoned comrades was dear old Dusty, the Flight Sergeant nominally responsible for Discipline;

a ripely Glaswegian character, not without his lovable side, who had set his heart on going to Paris and had been done out of his promised place at the last moment by the Machiavellian machinations of an Equipment Officer from a higher echelon, who presumably had more to offer.

Dusty was quite bitter about it, and to show his disgust immediately declared a moratorium on punishment, if not exactly on crime, and opened a housey-housey school forthwith. I remonstrated with the lad, but his sense of outrage outweighed his sense of duty. The notion of work was momentarily repugnant to him, though in the ordinary way he thoroughly enjoyed making other people do it.

'And anyway, the something so-and-so's snitched our last gallon of petrol,' he added as a clincher. I knew when I was beaten and gave up the unequal struggle, though an ingrained sense of guilt (for duty undone) struggled with an equally ingrained sense of outrage at the obtuseness of our betters. Once again the ostentatious self-indulgence of a privileged caste had undermined the sense of duty of those whose only privilege it was to serve. Will we never learn?

> Acts of injustice done
> Between the setting and the rising sun
> In history lie like bones, each one.

It crossed my mind to sit and join the school, but I felt that it might be better for ultimate discipline and good order to beat a dignified retreat. Besides, few had ever emerged from one of Dusty's schools with a clear profit. Many imagined they did, only to find later that Dusty had his own methods of recouping his temporary losses.

Instead I provoked a few of the more cautious and saving sort of sergeants into a quiet game of poker. There are moments when I know it is propitious for me to play this game of games. Such moments are few and far between; they are created by a certain tension of emotional cross-currents, which I have learned to recognise. When you feel circumstances are just too bizarre for rationality to cope with, a sort of clear detachment falls upon you; you feel uninvolved, a spectator, neither reckless nor cautious, beyond chance, an outsider looking in on a game that is too preposterous to be taken seriously. It is then that I cannot lose.

Nor did I lose now. I cleaned them out of their little hoards of Liberation money, and determined to spend it before they got it back.

The light was beginning to fail and I was sprucing up in the exiguous shelter of a groundsheet stretched tent-like along the side of the truck, a sort of lean-to of rubberised canvas, beneath which we should sleep. A man stepped up to me as I emerged to towel myself dry in the darkling air. He was a civilian, a shortish man but stocky, wearing an old suit and a beret and carrying a Sten gun.

'Bon soir, m'sieu,' he said.

'Bonne chance!' said I, thinking my God where are the bloody sentries?

The citizen of Beauvais, for such he was, invited me to accompany him to that pleasant town, which lay beneath us a mile or two distant. He said that he could procure us a good meal and a bottle of wine, and that he would be honoured to discuss *la guerre* with the distinguished sergeant. I saw to it that lookouts were indeed posted, and alert; spoke seriously to Dusty of his duties and the pregnant possibilities of laxity; promised to stand watch myself when I returned; and departed with my new friend.

He took me to a restaurant off the main square. It was the first time since well before D-day, the first time for months, and I had been in a restaurant or indeed in an intact and civilised town, unless you can count Bayeux, which was so cramped and swamped with soldiery that its civilian character was submerged. It was an unforgettable moment.

There were a few Allied officers present, but they, like the happy French civilians, were prepared to let a mere sergeant have his expansive moment, in this prevailing and somewhat premature mood of liberation. My friend introduced me to his friend the *patron*, and, pointing to my medal ribbon, which was no more than a modest statement to the initiated that I had 'got some in', gave me considerable build-up as a veritable hero of the liberation. I don't know what he thought I was doing hanging around Beauvais, in that case, but I let it slide. There is a time for modesty and a time for melodrama, and everything that was happening was so superbly melodramatic that it seemed curmudgeonly to correct him. We were all a little above ourselves, still living high on the breakthrough and the liberation of Paris.

My poker winnings came in handy to pay for the steak and wine which were consumed that night. One did not think of this gaudy confetti, printed for the Forces, as real money at all. It was with a sense of wonder that one saw it accepted, by apparently level-headed citizens, in return for real wine, real meat, real chips and mushrooms and tomatoes. Bottle after bottle came out, was passed around, consumed; toasts innumerable drunk. Unwontedly full of food, I remained quite sober; I didn't care much for the wine anyway. And my friend the citizen seemed perfectly impervious, though he put away his share.

It was late when I left, to keep my tryst at the laager. My new friend walked with me to the edge of the town. He had been regaling me with stories of the Resistance and the Occupation. At one point he touched my sleeve and stopped. It was a dark narrow street.

'J'ai tué,' he said impressively, 'deux Boches. L'un ici' – and he pointed dramatically to the cobbles at our feet – 'l'autre dans les bois où vous restez.'

'With the gun?' I asked, touching his Sten.

'No. With the knife. Before we got the guns.' And he whipped out a butcher's knife, thin with use and stoning. I felt its keen blade in the vague moonlight, and felt my feet sliding in blood that had long since dried on the ancient cobbles. I felt terribly sober and profoundly sad. The whole euphoria of the evening, the bitter gaiety of the day, dispersed in a moment of intense melancholy.

I said goodbye to the citizen on the borders of the country, where the shadowy woods loomed and leaned towards the town. He wrung my hand and wished me luck and turned back to the town, walking firmly, a sturdy and self-possessed figure, a man who had done what he felt necessary.

All night walking around the sleeping trucks I watched the dark woods and the shadowed town below. I felt that I should never sleep again. I slept at dawn, and as the day waxed I worked calmly on the machines, glad to be occupied with work that had no melodramatic aspect, but was commonplace and unsurprising, such as a man might do in a town at peace. We ate our biscuits and bully and brewed our tea, and in the evening several walked to town, but I felt that I had emancipated myself for the moment from melodrama, and stayed on site. I played poker and lost heavily, thinking of my momentary friend, to whom I had nothing more to say; nor he to me.

A family in Brabant

The Spitfire had crashed in a difficult position for us, in the corner of a field, hard up against a dyke, in Brabant in the Netherlands. In one respect we were fortunate, for it fell on the British side of the lines, which meant that the Germans had not had the opportunity of fixing it up with booby traps, or mining the approach we had to take to recover it. That was a relief. On the other hand it was tricky to approach with our recovery vehicles, especially since it had come to rest, after skidding across a field, with its propeller boss almost up against a tree. The pilot was a lucky man. The tip of his starboard wing overhung the water.

We worked hard that day, first manœuvring our crane into position, then our three-ton truck in which we kept our gear, and finally the long-loader which would carry the fuselage and wings back to base for our betters to put together again.

Afternoon was well advanced by the time we had dragged the Spitfire backwards into a more accessible position, and begun the tedious work of stripping off the fillets, disconnecting the meticulously locked control cables, and slacking off the split-pinned bolts which held the wings to the fuselage. We had been out from base since long before first light, on this gloomy December day in 1944, and so much time had been wasted in the laborious approach to the job that dusk took us by surprise with our task barely half-done.

It was plain that we should not get the Spitfire back to base that night, and we were too far away to think of returning for a night in the middle of a job – a thing we almost never did. The prospect of spending the long winter night in the vehicles was no more attractive than usual, but there seemed, in that lonely waste, little prospect of an alternative lodging. Then I recalled a small farmhouse a mile or so away, which we had seen across a couple of frozen fields during our circuitous approach to the desolate scene of the crash, which had previously existed in our minds only as a map reference, a figurative figment with no reality. I took the DR's motorcycle and made a reconnaissance, bumping over frozen ruts and sliding on the skim ice which was hardening as the light failed and the misty landscape of Brabant grew even more tenuous and inhospitable,

I was heartened to see a strong plume of smoke rising vertically from the chimney of the cottage – it was no more than a cottage, and the farm was no more than a smallholding. As I drew near a young girl closed the shutters across the parlour window, in which an oil lamp burned. The family were battening down for the night. The long sad night.

The farmer, a tall gangling man with grizzled hair, came to the door and listened gravely while I tried to make him understand that seven of us wanted shelter for the night. All his family were girls, five of them, ranging in age from about eight to about fifteen. Not the happiest prospect, I could understand, to have his lonely home invaded at dusk, with the long night ahead, by seven of the rude soldiery. But he took it well, though an amazing silence had fallen on the room behind him, his wife and five daughters speechless with surprise and, possibly apprehension. Then when he told them that guests were coming, what a buzz broke out!

He invited me in, to the living room with its gleaming red-tiled floor, with a good Dutch stove, a square kitchen table, wooden chairs and benches along the bare walls. He let me understand that we could spend the evening there, with the family, but we should have to sleep in the loft. We went up a ladder and I saw in the gleam of his lantern that the entire floor was covered with golden corn. He indicated that it could be swept up into a mound and I hoped that I had let him know that we would do that little chore ourselves. But when I returned with the lads, it had been done.

Many and many an evening we spent, during the campaign, with hosts who had not actually invited us, did not know we were coming; wonderful the hospitality of the Belgians and the Dutch, who had so little to give and gave it so willingly. But this is the night which stays in my memory most vividly, complete and perfect, a picture in the mind's eye like a Dutch interior, softly lit by lamplight and firelight, framed in gold.

My lads were a decent lot, though given to slanging matches among themselves which sometimes grew tedious. But they came mainly from decent homes, were sons or husbands of decent women, and I was always touched by their gentleness and chivalry towards the children and women whom we had come to liberate and who were living under such hard conditions.

We handed over what we had to give, indicating that the family should eat first while we cleaned up in the back kitchen at the pump, which was indoors. The merriment and wonder, how pathetic it was; yet, being human, we could not prevent ourselves from enjoying it. We gave them such treasures as bully beef, soap, coffee and chocolate, little enough in all conscience, but treasures unseen for far too long in Holland. Being country people with their own bit of land they naturally lived better than the poor people in the towns, but even so, all things are relative and their poverty after nearly five years of occupation was pretty dire. It was lovely to hear the children exclaiming and chattering in the next room, while we got our dirt off and spruced up in the cold back kitchen.

We brewed a great pot of tea and sat round drowsily, after we had eaten; smoking, sharing our tea and sweetmeats and tobacco, going through the difficult, frustrating and occasionally rewarding process of trying to communicate. They had no English and our Dutch was appallingly sketchy, and it looked like being a very long evening. Then suddenly, at a word from the mother, the little girls began to sing. Sitting in a row on a bench, with their backs to the wall and their elbows on the table; ranged in order of size, and presumably of age, the smallest near the stove.

They sang like angels, so unselfconsciously, looking straight ahead. It was perfectly obvious that they were used to doing this. As every song ended, and they looked at each other under lowered lashes and giggled nervously, while we applauded, their mother would pause for a moment, smiling shyly with gratification, then in a quiet voice would give them the next song, and off they would go again.

This was their entertainment. They sang every evening. I gathered that they were doing a few extra songs for our benefit, but they would have been singing anyway. What else was there to do?

There was nothing in that red-floored room except the stove, the table, a dresser, hard plain chairs and benches, two handwritten traditional exhortatory poems, naïvely illustrated, hanging on the wall in plain little frames, and a great big Bible standing on a sort of doodah which in England, in earlier times, might have borne an aspidistra.

They sang for the best part of an hour. Then father got to his feet and went over to the Bible. The little girls folded their hands in front of them and lowered their eyes. Father opened the big Bible and looked at us in a questioning sort of way. Everyone went quiet. Then he began to read.

He read three passages. I know that one was a psalm, one was a piece of Old Testament rhetoric, and one was from the New Testament. But I cannot identify them more particularly. It was a strange experience to hear him reading the Scriptures in his low Dutch voice.

He closed the Book and all the little girls, and their mother, folded their hands in the immemorial gesture of prayer. He said what was obviously an extempore prayer, standing by the big Bible with his eyes shut tight, his grizzled head bowed, his big rough peasant's hands hanging by his sides.

Then the little girls all trooped past us saying Good Night which is easy enough even in Dutch to understand. We all filed out to 'get a breath of fresh air' and ease ourselves in the frozen ditch. Our water and our breath steamed in the misty moonlight.

I suppose we were all in bed by nine o'clock or thereabouts. We lay on the polished boards of the floor of the loft, rolled in our blankets, inhaling the scent of the corn, the scent of all the harvests that had been stored there through the generations of war and peace.

In the morning we clattered down the almost vertical ladder to find the stove being roused and everyone active. It was a bracing quick wash in water that trembled on the brink of being ice, but we were rich today, there was steaming coffee for everyone and to spare, and bread and fat to eat.

The whole family came out to wave us goodbye when we clambered into the truck. The first light was just beginning to steal across the fields, flat fields of Brabant white with frost, sweating with mist. The light came stealing reluctantly, from the enemy's country, towards which we turned our faces now.

They were all lined up by the yard gate, and still the little girls kept station, tallest on the right, shortest on the left. It was as if they felt themselves a unit, and their unity was important to them, in that lonely waste. They raised their hands and waved and their voices like bells came to us over the crackle of heavy tyres on frosty earth as the wheels began to turn.

'*Tot straks!*' they cried. '*Tot siens!*' Till we meet again. But we were never to return.

Luftwaffe pilot

Gunfire woke me. It was already light. A thin cold wintry light. I was sleeping on the tiled floor of a cellar. The building had been ruined by bombs. The walls lived to a few feet above the ground level, ragged chaos of rubble. I rolled out of my blankets and pushed my feet into gumboots and snatched up the Sten gun and raced up the half-dozen stairs, out into the morning.

A fighter-bomber with black crosses on the underwing was coming in low towards the airfield. A Messerschmitt 109 with a bomb slung beneath the fuselage. It was pointing at me. How slow it seemed. I raised the Sten to fire and squeezed the trigger. Nothing happened. I had the safety catch on. The bomb was released and began to glide towards me. I pushed the safety catch off and aimed at the bomb. As I fired with all my faith, praying bullets, it dawned on me that the bomb was not a bomb. It was a drop tank, an auxiliary petrol tank which the German had just jettisoned. It floated down slowly.

Everything seemed to be happening with extreme slowness and deliberation, as in a dream. I dismissed the dream-bomb from my nervous system and swung round to fire after the aircraft, which was going in now towards the airstrip. I emptied my magazine at it. It went over in some firs and I knew where it was heading.

I dashed down the stairs again, snatched up my tin hat and spare magazines, and raced through the firs, along the path we used, towards the strip. I was not conscious of strain.

When I came through to the strip that ran between the dark firs the battle was almost over. The Bofors guns of the Regiment were hacking away, a big Canadian sergeant-major was standing out on the strip with a Bren gun firing it like a rifle, from his shoulder. The mechanics around the revetments and dispersals were firing with anything, if they had anything; lying down, kneeling, sometimes running across from one unsafe place to another in that awkward stooping crouch men adopt at such times, as if taken short. Some of our aircraft were burning. The

Germans kept on coming in, a squadron of Messerschmitts crossing and turning, beating up the dispersals with heavy cannon fire.

But the Bofors guns were getting to them now, and the twenty-
millimetre light AA guns on those swinging cradles were putting
up vivid deadly arcs and fans of fire.

It went quiet for a weird moment then a lone Messerschmitt
drove down along the runway, parallel with the ground, doing
perhaps 300 miles an hour, with cannon sparks winking at us as he
fired his guns. Everyone had him in the sights for a fraction of
time; Bren, Sten, Bofors, twenty-millimetre guns, rifles.... Suddenly he seemed to shimmer brightly, and shudder. The nose
dipped and the whirling propeller scraped the runway, and smoke,
then a flicker of flame, came from the cowlings. He skidded
along for a bit then veered, lurching, rocking, bouncing. He
skated off the runway on to the grass. He shuddered to a stop.

It was over.

We were busy for a time looking after our own, clearing up the
mess; it was some time before I approached the Messerschmitt.
For some reason it had not burned badly. The fire had gone out
before it consumed the pilot. I can't remember now just why,
but of course there was a good credible technical reason. I remember his legs were scorched but his body seemed unscathed.
He had an erection. He lay back in his seat with his eyes open,
dead, staring past us, beyond the dark firs, beyond the wintry
Dutch landscape towards the Fatherland, which was so near,
just a few miles distant, over the River Maas.

He was very young.

I wondered if he was the one who had woken me up. (I had
been off-duty that morning, having worked half the night. That's
why I was alone in the ruined cellar which I shared with three
others).

Whether he was the one, or another, it was all the same. We
had tried to kill each other, and now he was dead. The odds were
against him.

We got him out and handed him over and dragged the enemy
aircraft away to be examined by our boffins. We worked like
dogs that day, getting the strip cleared and ready for action
again. We had lost quite a few aircraft. It was the Luftwaffe's last
throw, or near enough. It shook us. But we were fully operational
again before darkfall.

There was some whisky drunk in the sergeants' mess that night.

When we turned the Tilley lamp out in the cellar and got our heads down three of us fell asleep almost at once, we were all dead beat, but the fourth lay for a long time staring into the darkness, seeing a very young German's face, white as death, staring back, staring past me, staring through me, staring into the terrible dark void of death.

Colonel, Sir

I took the Harley-Davidson to reconnoitre. We had the map reference for where the rocket-firing Typhoon had crashed, but this was strange country, between Eindhoven and Nijmegen, we were strangers in it. The army had forced a corridor up to the Maas and Lower Rhine, but it was narrow and precarious, the road got cut, and although we had sent a detachment to the airfield at Grave the situation was what is known as fluid. I thought I'd better spend a little time in spying out the land before we committed the heavy recovery vehicles which we had assembled on the ruined airfield of Volkel.

I was burbling along this narrow road, enjoying the feel of being on a motorcycle again, when I began to get an uneasy feeling that the atmosphere was not quite right. Occasionally you got this eerie feeling; too quiet, not enough vehicles and people in sight.

Suddenly there were six little explosions along the verge of this quiet country road, fifty yards ahead of me and travelling away. It was a stick of mortar bombs. They burst in a neat row of smokey puffs on the left-hand verge. I stopped the bike and looked round. Six more burst behind me. There was a house on an S-bend in the road just ahead of the first bursts. I let in the clutch and headed for it. I wanted to tell somebody that this was quite unfair, I hadn't been trained for close contact with the enemy infantry, I'm a mechanic you know, practically a noncombatant. Then I thought you *have* been trained, you know, think of all those battle courses.... As I swung off the road into the little orchard by the cottage there were more bangs. Tiles clattered off the roof into the road and a tall sergeant-major came running out and belted round the house and into the field beyond, on the right-hand side, where the bombs were coming from.

There was a jeep parked up against the house, in the orchard, and a lieutenant-colonel, hatless, with streaks of dirt on his face, was talking into a radio, or perhaps it was a field-telephone, I forget. His driver and another soldier stood waiting for him, holding their Sten guns at the ready. I unslung mine.

The colonel hung up and gave me a charming smile. He was very young, I thought, to hold that rank. A boy in his twenties.

'Don't see many of you airmen up here,' he said, but he said it pleasantly. He turned to his soldiers. 'All right,' he said, 'they're on the job. We'll go and watch. Coming, sergeant?'

He led the way along the wall of the house and over to the garden boundary. There was a wet ditch and a fence. He leaned nonchalantly against the fence. The soldiers got down in the ditch.

'There they are,' the colonel said, pointing across a narrow strip of field to the far hedge. 'I saw them then.'

'A bit cheeky, colonel, sir,' one of the soldiers said.

'Very,' said the colonel. 'But we'll nip them out. They will regret it. You see there, sergeant' – he gestured to the right – 'our chaps are coming in there, any moment now.' He was wholly calm.

A few more mortar bombs fell near us, then came a long burst of Bren gun fire across the fields, followed by the plop of more distant mortars – ours? – and ragged firing from small arms. An Auster artillery spotting plane came trudging across the field towards the cottage, and soon afterwards the crumps of twenty-five-pounder shells exploding. Smoke drifted across the meadows and I heard the rumble of tanks.

A runner came to call the colonel back to the radio, or field telephone. We all strolled back to the cottage as if we had been doing a bit of gardening. The colonel tapped my breast pocket. 'What have you there, sergeant?'

'Frederick Prokosch, *Chosen Poems*, sir. My wife just sent them out.'

To my surprise he stopped and said,

> Music, the lion, the legendary day
> All go, these swallows from the lasting sky
> Forever fall and fall and fall away,
> The torrent fails, the natural fountains die ...

'Colonel, sir,' the soldier called, at the phone

'I'm going on up,' the colonel said when he had finished on the blower. 'All right, corporal.'

His driver got in and started the jeep and turned it. The colonel got in beside him.

'Where are you heading for, sergeant?' he called. I told him.

'Better follow us, then. Can't have the Air Force getting lost on the field of battle.' He smiled that boyish smile.

'The airman soars....' I said. He took it up:

> The airman soars and through our humming blood
> Saunter the fugue, the carnival, and love ...

'Get rolling!'

I kicked the big Harley to life and turned out of the orchard after the jeep. The road twisted and turned and every so often there was a R.A.S.C. truck in the ditch, shot up and burned. After a while we came to a fork. The jeep slowed to a stop and the colonel waved me down. I came alongside him.

'You take the high road and we'll take the low road,' the colonel said. Actually they were both low roads. But he meant me to take the left fork while he went right, towards the battle. Consulting his map, he gave me precise instructions.

'I'm very much obliged to you, colonel, sir.'

'My pleasure,' said the colonel. 'I too had the new Prokosch sent out. Wish we had time to discuss it. Give my regards to the Tactical Air Force, won't you?'

There was a bitter rending crack and an 88-millimetre shell burst a few yards up the tree-lined road he was to take.

'Get weaving, sergeant!'

The jeep leaped forward and carried him towards the battle, the dark woods and the bitter road.

He was only a boy, younger than me, a boy with easy manners and a lively mind and a sense of duty that transcended fear. I hope he came through all right. I hope he lived to read some more in the little book we both carried, sent out by someone who understood.

> Birds flow under the heavens,
> And seas over their bed,
> And the endless sea of history
> Flows over the dead.

13

Some Editors

THE day after I was demobilised I had luncheon at the Savoy Grill with Herbert Gunn, who was then Editor of the London *Evening Standard*. I decided against wearing my chalk-striped grey 'flannel' demob suit – wisely, I'm sure – and turned up in my only wearable pre-war suit, with the wide trousers and double-breasted jacket. It wasn't quite Savoy Grill, but then, neither was I. What little social savoir-faire I ever had had been eroded by five and a half years in the ranks of the R.A.F., where I served as an airframe fitter, or at least that was my grade, though I did less actual *fitting* than most fitters. Demolition, organisation, administration, and exhortation were more in my line, and I have no doubt that my relatively swift promotion to the dizzy rank of sergeant was largely due to my usefulness to various senior officers as a sort of unofficial adjutant or mouthpiece, for I composed in my time many eloquent and guileful letters, memoranda, speeches and notices, all of which carried someone else's signature. I have always quite enjoyed 'ghosting' and have written many thousands of words in other people's personae. There is a subtle pleasure in doing this; one becomes a kind of dramatist in real life.

When the Second Front was approaching and I had to get down to actual work on actual aeroplanes these quasi-literary activities came sharply to an end, and I must say I enjoyed my life in the 2nd Tactical Air Force a great deal more than my previous static and boring years on operational training units of Fighter Command. I never got to like either aircraft or fitting, but the rough rackety life of action and movement, the sense of adventure and proximity of the enemy, while it gave one many a pang, did approximate more closely to the life one had expected, did seem to have some point and purpose and was frequently quite exciting.

My skill as a craftsman having been quite accurately estimated by my officers, I was relieved of the necessity of doing any actual precision fitting and was put in charge of a salvage gang, briefed to hare off into the blue and recover our fighter aircraft when they were shot down, bringing them back to base for better men to repair them. Needless to say, this was a reflection on my skill as a craftsman, but since it was entirely justified I never resented it. I was on the contrary much relieved. Except when I was frightened or deeply depressed by the sights one saw, I actually enjoyed this carefree bohemian life, lived far away from head-quarters and mainly in close contact with the army, among whom our aircraft tended to fall. We wore khaki battledress and considered ourselves a cut above the base wallahs, who in their turn regarded us as irresponsible roughnecks; though not without a touch of envy, I fancy. I spent my leisure in editing and writing a satirical unit magazine which was popular with everyone except our officers.

However, entertaining and educative as this life undoubtedly was, it could hardly be considered a perfect preparation for luncheon at the Savoy Grill and high executive office in the London *Evening Standard*. I had never had much talent as a man-about-town, and when one of my future colleagues on the *Standard* said to me, with an air of languid superiority, 'This is the boulevardier's paper, y'know,' I realised that I was up the creek without a paddle, yet again.

I had arrived on the *Evening Standard* quite by accident; one of the many inadvertencies which have made my life so interesting. I should have gone back to the *Daily Express*, but when, in the later stages of the war, Bertie Gunn succeeded Michael Foot who had succeeded Frank Owen, as Editor of the *Standard*, he asked me if I'd like to work with him in Shoe Lane, instead of going back to the black glasshouse in Fleet Street. I had got on well with Gunn when he was successively Night Editor and Managing Editor of the *Express*, and replied that certainly, I'd be delighted. When one is stuck on the wrong side of the Rhine, surrounded by an alien and deeply hostile population, one is so chuffed to hear talk of actual jobs to go back to, in Civvy Street, that one doesn't feel particularly fastidious. I liked Bert, I hadn't really enjoyed the *Express* so very much, after all my expectations, and I was very pleased to return to evening newspaper hours. They start awfully early, but they knock off at a civilised hour and leave you free to live a normal sort of life in the evenings; assuming that's what you want, of course. Not everybody does.

I have done a lot of night work in my time and though I personally am far from enamoured of it, I do understand that to some people it is a heavenly substitute for having to live a normal life and enjoy yourself in the evening. There *is* something in being on the job when everyone else is free, and vice versa. You feel superior, in a word; either masochistically a martyr, which appeals so deeply to some temperaments, or just on your tod, off the hook of normal domesticity. Either way, if it happens to appeal to you, you are *different*, a member of an élite, a crank who is socially justified in his crankiness, the object of (misplaced) sympathy, which is so nice, and, what is more, free to while away your afternoons outrageously while most people are slowly sinking to the day's lowest point of fretfulness and frustration. But for me, normality was preferred. I still thought I *was* normal. Well, I had my doubts, and with reason, but I still felt I *should* be, and strove against the grain of my nature to achieve this.

Bertie had no doubts that he was normal, and no reason to have doubts. I think he was very normal. But not, of course, *ordinary*. People who pride themselves on their normality do not pride themselves on their ordinariness, as a rule. (Though Sir Lew Grade is one who does.) Bert had come up in the ordinary way through local journalism, somewhere in Kent if I recall, and most of his experience had been at the sub-editors' end of the business, which throws up more high executives than the writing end, I fancy. He was a sound reporter and a first-rate sub-editor, one of the very best. In fact he was one of nature's chief sub-editors and at that level he was quite outstanding. But like so many others, he was quite naturally promoted out of his real métier. He was very effective as Night Editor of the *Express*, and when Chris was ill for a fairly long period he stood in quite ably, in charge of the whole paper. But of course in wartime he didn't have to reveal all the qualities that a good editor is made of; the scope was much restricted, there was virtually no inspirational hiring and firing and long-range planning and big promotional thinking. It was a case of jogging along and keeping the machine ticking over in its well-established bright crisp way. This Bertie was thoroughly well qualified to do.

But the jobs of Managing Editor of the *Daily Express* and Editor of the *Evening Standard* could scarcely have been more different. Perhaps I ought to explain, for the benefit of readers unaccustomed to the terminology, that although to lay eyes the term Managing Editor may look grander than Editor, in practice the Managing Editor is a manager rather than an editor, a dogs-body serving the Editor as a sort of adjutant, administrator, trouble-shooter, section leader, or simply an assistant. He has a vital role in the production of the paper but less say in policy-making, appointments and the general direction than the Editor, to whom he must answer. He is usually, if not invariably, waiting to become Editor himself; though there are some weary old Managing Editors who have enough sense to realise that they would not really enjoy it and who are merely awaiting retiring age, which seems long a-coming. You have to pass your expenses through the Managing Editor, and if for no other reason than that he is often regarded with something almost indistinguishable from awe. In platoon terms, he is the sergeant to the Editor's subaltern. This is sometimes a strict and close analogy. I thought I might elucidate this point since in business a Managing Director has it over the mere Director, whereas, as you now understand, an Editor has it all over a mere Managing Editor.

The word editor is misleading at several points. In a general sense people who write don't edit, and people who edit don't write. There are mere sub-editors, who handle news or sporting copy, and features sub-editors who handle articles, then you crawl up the hierarchy through beings like sports editors, features editors, literary editors, chief sub-editors, who govern the news sub-editors, and then on up where the air gets thin (and some-times the ideas get thinner), through assistant editors, production editors, managing editors right on up to editors proper, editors absolute. There are many anomalies which destroy that neat logical breakdown which I have just given you. Some writers are rewarded late in life with the title of associate editor, which means whatever it is meant to mean, and there are even con-sultant editors which is also a flexible term. There *are* editors who write, just to prove my generalisation unsound; though I'm not sure I'd admit that there are writers who edit. In America they call great numbers of people editor – Radio Editor, TV Editor, Motoring Editor, and so on. This must be done to give pleasure and the illusion of prestige. It is all part of the galloping devaluation of words. We used to call such contributors corres-pondents, but that doesn't flatter the job enough. These days people want money, prestige, status, *and* perks. And many of them use the newspaper, which in the old days used to have an absolute prior claim on one's loyalty, as merely first base, the necessary but rather boring peg, on which to hang other remunerative and glamorous jobs such as appearing on television, or in advertisements and commercials, or in glossy magazines. Things ain't only not what they used to be; they're worse, except that we all pay ourselves a lot more, which I must admit is nice.

Well, as I was saying, Bertie found it quite a change when he became Editor of the *Evening Standard*; and I found it quite a change too, when I left the Air Force, lunched with him at the Savoy Grill, and emerged as his Features Editor. In those days the *Standard* was a slightly depressed and depressing little paper with a smaller circulation than it liked among people who fancied themselves a cut above the *hoi polloi* who bought the *Star* in fair numbers and the *Evening News* in very considerable numbers. When the *Star* and its parent, the *News Chronicle*, folded in the 'Fifties, the *News* went right on growing, picking up circulation effortlessly through its sheer mediocrity, which was so in tune with the mediocrity of the population who bought it, and the *Standard* went on struggling in this curious role of intelligent, with-it, boulevardier's paper. It is now under the Editorship of Charles Wintour very much less depressing – and less depressed, I should imagine, judging by all those massed pages of close-packed advertisements.

Faced with the stimulating challenge of bringing the *Standard* forward into the peacetime 'Forties, Bert thrashed about manfully, applying his considerable technical know-how to no great purpose, since what the paper wanted was not so much a face-lift as a fresh energising philosophy and preferably a team of new writers. It went short of the first but gradually acquired the second, including Milton Shulman, Kenneth Tynan and Charles Wintour. It was quite a struggle, in the course of which (while it lasted) Bertie gave several fascinating performances as the great editor, his favourite role.

He was really a very down-to-earth and practical person, of Scottish extraction, but like everyone else he had his dreams and one of them was the dream of the great Beaverbrook tycoon-editor. Beaverbrook was bossy and impish, as is well known, and having a considerable knowledge of what made men tick and a somewhat cynical evaluation of human motives he used to pay his top executives generously, accustom them to high living, urge them on to live up to their new positions, and then play mercilessly on their quite natural dread of suddenly being dropped from a great height into the dunghill on which most people crawled. He was always interfering and he interfered brutally at times, reducing strong men to the brink of tears. His tyranny never cut any ice with me, I used to laugh at it, it was so palpably absurd and gnomish. But then, of course, I never expected or desired high promotion and was to that extent invulnerable. Having seen what 'success' could mean, I should think not. Bertie was given the treatment, and although quite tough-fibred he suffered quite a bit. Like so many others who suffer themselves from bullying, he in his turn tried to come the old acid at times with those who served under him. He could be very bitchy though I must say he could also be very kind and sympathetic, and I got on with him quite well for quite a time. But with Bertie, you never knew just what mood he would be in.

Invariably he was in a gloomy mood first thing. One really couldn't blame him. Our first editorial conference was called around 8.30 a.m., if memory serves; some such ghastly hour. No one feels at his best at such an hour, surely? With the possible exception of devoted keep-fit revivalists. But the early conference was at least consistent: Bert was *never* very happy. Around eleven we all used to push off for a quick nip at the pub across

the road. When I say we all, I must be insulting somebody's
unsullied memory and record, so I will change it to some of us
used to nip out. Bertie's couple of quick gins did him a power of
good, it was delightful to see him visibly thawing and becoming
human. This habit of the mid-morning snifter was probably very
bad for me; I simply loved it but didn't really know when to
stop (when *do* you stop?) and until I took a grip on myself I
was becoming quite a mid-morning soak. I don't say I'm nicer
to know now that I've kicked it, but at least I'm *me*, dependable
old Mo, sober and God how boring.

More often than not Bertie would go out to lunch, with someone important or celebrated of course, and as often as not at the
Savoy Grill or some place on that sort of level. He invariably came
back happy and buoyant. I do not mean drunk. I never saw him
even slightly drunk in all the years I knew him. He could carry
his liquor better than almost anyone I ever knew. But naturally
the outing had an effect, if only to make him buoyant, genial and
optimistic. This was well known to one and all and there were
those who thought they had a system for putting in small requests
at the best moment.

But the interesting thing was the effect conviviality had on
Bertie's judgment, of people and of ideas and of writing. A bad
idea at 8 a.m. sometimes became a good idea at 11.30. A very
good idea at 3 p.m. became a stinker at 5 p.m. I never knew
anyone change more quickly, unless it was my mother, who
made inconsistency a guessing game. Two hours was enough to
produce a different man. Yet, as I have stressed, he never got
drunk, not even tipsy. He was simply elevated, or alternatively
cast down. I failed over the years to form an opinion as to whether
his judgment was sounder when elevated, or when cast down.
But to those of us who were on the receiving end, his sudden
alternations between elevation and depression could be slightly
trying.

I was nominally responsible for the features, but Bertie interfered all the time and I quickly lost interest and jacked it in to
become a columnist. I wasn't very good at it, anyway. I had lost
what flair I ever had. I had the sad duty of passing on to George
Orwell Bertie's views about the column he was then writing,
every Saturday. Bert wanted him to write about more trivial,
homely and 'human' subjects; 'human' was a great word and

when you heard it coming out you ducked. At one time he was quite obsessed with getting Orwell to write about how to make a nice pot of tea. He was totally out of sympathy with Orwell's cast of mind, of course. I tried to persuade Orwell to carry on writing his column, even if it meant occasionally relaxing and meeting Gunn halfway. But after a few weeks he simply couldn't take any more and told me, quite nicely, that he would finish that week.

When I reported back to Bert he flew into a panic. He might not enjoy Orwell or even begin to understand him, but he knew he was a name to be reckoned with, and he knew Beaverbrook knew; and to lose him – so different from sacking him – was unthinkable. 'I charge you to keep him on the paper,' he boomed at me during conference. Beaverbrook executives sometimes picked up these pompous, old-fashioned and often quasi-biblical expressions from the old man. 'I *charge* you to keep him.' But the Charge of the Light Brigade wouldn't have kept him.

Ronald Duncan, that very considerable poet, playwright, and man of letters, was another who found it difficult to work for us, though I believe he had the Old Man's blessing. Bertie couldn't see how best to use this brilliant young man, who drifted about, small and gentle and quite without the superficial 'glamour' which Bert could recognise. He wanted to write satire, he murmured. This threw Bert into a tizzy of dubiety. 'Satire ... a very tricky business,' he said. 'Doesn't work on newspapers, you know.' He recommended that he should write something about carpets.

'But I don't know anything about carpets,' said Ronald.

'Nor care, I should think,' said I.

Bert darted me a venomous glance and withdrew to his sanctum. Later he gave me instructions to get Duncan writing – about carpets. Of course I never did. Another writer who could have been a treasure to us, a writer who had not only dazzling power over words, but a headful of ideas, a fascinated interest in the society that was evolving after the war, was lost to the paper.

I myself tried to write a weekly column of pertinent comment on the way life was going, a column with some ideas in it, some relevance to the seething cauldron of change in which we were all simmering; but he wouldn't have it, though I've never written better, or to more point and purpose. He was afraid of ideas. He

was the right man for the *Express*, all froth and bubble, facile
optimism and underlying profound distrust of the emergent
society and the forces that were shaping it.

When he was not being very unkind to me, he was being very
kind. He was a charming host with a charming wife and nice
clever family. I liked him a lot, and I think he liked me until I
began to get stubborn, or 'difficult', as he put it; but as the years
went by it became more and more obvious that we were cut of
different cloth, and when I decided to leave he to took my
defection as a personal affront (which perhaps it was). We parted
icily. He used to boast that some journalists called him 'the most
ruthless bastard in Fleet Street'. I don't think he was, but he
liked to think so.

As soon as I had left Bert's employ, I began to regret him. He
was fairly difficult as a boss, in this sense that you never quite
knew what mood he would be in and had to gauge your approach
accordingly, a sort of gambler's approach which made new ideas
even more tricky to handle than they usually are. (And they
always are.) But the good times were very good and both on and
off duty we had some rare frolics and capers, and above all that,
you knew you were dealing with a tough old pro who knew the
ins and outs of the game backwards, within the rules, even if he
was a bit of a philistine reactionary by some delicate standards.

Some time later, I was co-opted on to the staff of *The Sunday
Times* as a writer. I began by writing a little piece weekly about
fishing; this developed into a weekly essay on country matters
generally, and before long I was appointed Television and Radio
Critic and turned my back on the executive life for ever.

I have worked for four Editors of *The Sunday Times*, since
1949. The first was W. W. Hadley – 'Pop' – who was well over
eighty. He was a nice simple old boy who was proud to recall
his weekly meetings with Neville Chamberlain when that
mediocrity was Prime Minister. He had kept the attenuated paper
going through the war and in a nice old-fashioned way he had
good judgment, but plainly he was hardly the man to take the
paper forward into the fearful 'Fifties, and he was retired *cum
laude* and replaced by H. V. Hodson. Before he died I used to
visit Pop in his retirement bungalow near Hindhead, where he
lived very modestly, surrounded by his books and (doubtless)
memories. You would never think he had been Editor of *The*

Sunday Times, but he was a sweet-natured old boy with great natural dignity and we got on nicely.

I should value five minutes with him now, to get his views on *The Sunday Times* of today. I think he might refuse to surface even if given the opportunity.

Harry Hodson was perhaps the most striking Editor the paper has had. He was about as tall as Bertie Gunn, built on the same greyhound lines, and equally well dressed though in a quite different and distinctive style. While Bertie was always poured into the nattiest line in navy blue or light grey suiting, usually pin-striped, Harry favoured a magisterial style. He usually or at any rate he often wore a black coat and striped 'sponge bag' trousers, and invariably a black hat, either a Homburg (the 'Anthony Eden') or a bowler. He was even better-looking than Bert, a real classical good-looker; while Bertie had straight silver hair that was slicked down flat in the Brylcreem manner of his period, Harry had wavy silver hair that helped to give him a look of the greatest distinction. But he really did have distinction. He had been a Brackenbury Scholar of Balliol and a Fellow of All Souls. He was a very fine academic who had missed the vulgar hurly-burly of rough-and-tumble journalism but was no worse for that, I dare say. He was a member of the Athenaeum and had high political contacts. He was an expert on India. We all believed that Harold Macmillan would give him a peerage, or at the very least a knighthood, and it was a disappointment, to me at any rate, that Macmillan did not. He would have graced the House of Lords and might yet. I hope so. It would prove his métier.

Under Harry's direction the paper made great progress and I was very happy in my work. We had one or two, not more than two, high barneys, but by and large got on well. I respected his judgment and he taught me to write more carefully than I was prone to write. This was not by any means wholly bad for me. I *needed* the gently restraining influence of a father-figure, a man whose literacy I could respect and who would by his example tend to tone down my wilder flights.

Harry only once refused to print something which I had written. It was his right. I have always believed that an editor has no right to make you write anything you don't want to write, but has an absolute, if negative, right to refuse to publish anything he doesn't want to publish. This negative right is very important to the health of publications. It is not tyrannical. If the writer is wholly out of sympathy with the editor, he should go elsewhere where he will feel more at home. But an editor must set the tone of his paper – if he doesn't, who will? – and though of course he shouldn't be constantly niggling and fiddling around with his contributors' copy, he can refuse to print it and the writer can refuse to remain in his team. If it happens often enough, then obviously the writer and the editor just don't belong on the same staff. All the good editors I have worked for have given me (and my colleagues) great freedom.

The bit that Harry jibbed at was a swingeing attack I made on Sir Ian Jacobs, who was then Director-General of the BBC. I think it was really rather too intemperate and nowadays I should put it differently. That apart, Harry helped me considerably by reading my copy every Friday morning with scrupulous attention – those were the days! – and he was generous in his praise when I had made a good job of it. This is terribly important to a writer, even a newspaper writer, who is after all an artist *manqué* and should be allowed the tatters of artistic pride, boring though that is to all concerned.

Harry was not invariably wildly enthusiastic, of course – I recall, for example, that he was a much keener or perhaps I should say a more generous fan of Jimmy Edwards than I was, and it saddened him when I failed to share his pleasure in that robust comedian. But there were very few occasions indeed on which he felt it necessary to question my actual judgment: it was understood that a reviewer exercised his own judgment uninfluenced. Apart from my intemperate piece about Sir Ian Jacob, which I admit was ill-judged, he never objected to my views as such, but he was invariably helpful about the minutiae of presentation, intricate and beguiling questions of grammar and expression, on which he was a scholar and no doubts about that.

I learned quickly that when my stuff was good Harry would express his pleasure and even admiration, succinctly but generously: a tremendous tonic which invariably sent me out into the musty corridors of the old Kemsley House suffused with joy, elevated beyond my usual diffident state. If, on the other hand, Harry's reaction was tepid, perfunctory, a mere 'All right, Maurice,' then I knew that I had fallen below my own best

standard. Since I respected his judgment and probity, these
circumstances conspired to make me work hard at my column,
a thing which was not invariably good for it – sometimes spon-
taneity was ironed out by too much fastidious brooding – but at
any rate it was a case of one craftsman working hard to satisfy
the judgment of another.

All in all it was a very satisfactory relationship, though not
very close, not very intimate or personal. It was almost entirely
an office relationship: Bert Gunn was in fact the last editor whom
I knew on home-visiting terms, family terms. People who knew
him better told me that Harry could be quite a gay lad at parties,
and this I can well believe, for he had considerable social flair,
a sparkle in his handsome eye, exquisite manners, and basic
optimism. But in office affairs he was generally rather serious; as
well he might be. All in all, we got on well, though I fancy that
he began to discern that my views on the social structure were
unsound, as well they may be. At times, sickened by the obvious
mediocrity of the mediocre, I swung to an extreme and became
wildly élitist; at other times, influenced by my upbringing and
the suffering I had seen as a boy and young man, I veered towards
democracy. Harry was a natural member of the élite and vastly
steadier than me, though actually more tolerant, not less, of
actual inadequacy. So the relationship was at times uneasy
because we did not perhaps really understand each other perfectly. Sometimes I suspected snobbery and sometimes he
suspected egalitarianism. But there was a healthy mutual respect
going most of the time, Harry was very kind to me and very
helpful and I was in full support of his general attitude as an
editor, he conducted the paper on what I usually thought were
sound lines and certainly during his regime the literary and
arts side was at its best and the leader page a model. When I
heard that he was leaving us to become Provost of Ditchley I was
really sad.

He was the last Editor who found the time (and thought it
proper) to read my weekly offering himself, as I handed it in,
and to discuss it with me. I worked to him directly, without any
intermediary. Though we did not know it at the time, this phase
was the last kick of the old world, the pre-glossy magazine, pre-
big business, pre-diversification world; the dying moments of the
intimate, personal newspaper world of my youth, a world of

flair rather than calculation, of personal value judgments rather than mechanised commercial judgments, of insight rather than market research, of people rather than computers. I still regret it.

H. V. Hodson was succeeded as Editor by Denis Hamilton, who had long been a key figure in our establishment: Editorial Director first to Lord Kemsley and then to Lord Thomson, master of the big provincial empire and a powerful figure in the big London empire too. Denis had been a Territorial soldier in the Durham Light Infantry – his pre-war experience was wholly provincial – who rose to the rank of Brigadier at the age of twenty-six; which says much for his character and singleness of purpose. He was not a working journalist in the old sense of one who actually fiddles around obsessedly with words and pages, but he had far-ranging vision and drive that were made available precisely at that historic moment when it was believed that the paper had either to make a great leap forward into a new world, or mark time and (possibly) slip back. It was under his aegis that we grew mighty and enormous. He had been responsible for the great success of the war-time memoirs which helped to set us on the new road, he saw the colour magazine established and the division of the paper into those several specialist sections which have changed its character while making it immensely weightier, a far bigger business.

Harry Hodson's *Sunday Times* was still fundamentally a compact paper of authoritative comment, well informed, well written, with a clear political identity (enlightened Conservatism) and a distinct leaning towards literature and the arts. It had changed, of course; it had improved; but it was still essentially an unashamedly élitist organ of information and balanced comment which might well appeal to educated readers who cherished certain clearly established common standards of conduct and judgment. Denis Hamilton's *Sunday Times* moved forward, with television and the motor industry, into the expansion of affluence, with more emphasis on material satisfactions, more sympathy with the aspirations of the rising generation of easy-money big-spenders who were so set on keeping down with the Joneses, and a good deal less certainty that the standards of the so-called 'mandarin' classes were still valid or relevant.

Mr Hamilton has, above all, the gift of large-scale organisation and of looking continually forward into a future which I for one would just as soon ignore. He soon changed the *feel* of working on *The Sunday Times*; a fairly sensitive person became aware that it was becoming a vast juggernaut of an enterprise, sectionalised and compartmented, in which even the most self-assertive could not feel unduly important. I imagine that American Sunday papers may feel something like this. My personal connection with the paper began to become more tenuous. Though I still dutifully took in my column every Friday morning, I had lost my immediate, personal access to the Editor and had to hand my stuff to a succession of underlings, some of whom were not wholly congenial. The personal contact means so much. At length, after some unhappy times, I began to work directly to the Literary Editor, J. W. Lambert, and became happy again forthwith. But the Editor had become a remotely engrossed, tycoonlike executive, immersed in tremendous great projects and decisions, far too occupied to be concerned with details like reading my copy and discussing it with me. Of course he was absolutely right: the thing had changed and was changing all the time and the boss had to stand back from the detail and be a great organiser, administrator and delegator. It was the only way. We were heading into a new enlarged affluence, with its concomitant risks, and the man at the helm had to be a different sort of man, a man running a great business and occupied with far weightier decisions than the arrangement of the words in a given writer's column. I see this, I saw it then, I do not and did not dispute its rightness. I'm merely saying that for the individual writer and commentator, or at any rate for this one, the feel of the thing changed: the individual writer's relationship with his Editor became remoter.

How dear old Ben would have approved of Denis Hamilton! 'Thinking big,' planning forward, opening-up new territories, always expanding, setting on new staff including new young lions of whom the highest hopes were entertained ... it was Ben's dream-world, and it was inevitable, and it prospered mightily. Denis took his time to make up his mind, he wouldn't be rushed, but when he made a decision he stuck to it, he supported his chosen men, he took calculated risks and he saw us through into the new era. I doubt if anyone else could have done it.

He was always nice to me, though I think I must have been a bit of a puzzle to him, from time to time. I looked on him as a

big brother and he treated me generously, as indeed he did everyone. He is a generous man with a strong sense of justice. We
had only one serious barney about my television column, when
I went bald-headed for an edition of Huw Wheldon's *Monitor*
which was devoted to pop art. I wasn't so much attacking *Monitor*
as attacking pop art, which I thought degenerate. It was about
the time when life in Britain was approaching that watershed, a
crisis of confidence in itself and in traditional values: when so
many babies were being thrown out along with the bath-water.
We were very affluent and very uncertain. The Fringe, Profumo,
TW3, and after them the worst vulgarities of the permissive
society, were all approaching. Sensing the deluge to come, I was
at my most reactionary as I strove to dam the flood of juvenile,
ill-considered, thoroughly deleterious junk which was taking over.
I wanted change and I want it still, but I am a gradualist, I want
to conserve the best of the old while selecting and welcoming the
best of the new. I upbraided *Monitor* for taking this pop art
rubbish too seriously. On the Saturday afternoon I was telephoned
at our cottage in Sussex by Pat Murphy, then Managing Editor.
He told me that Mr Hamilton was upset and reluctant to print
my stuff, on the grounds that I had gone too far, had made myself
sound like a 'reactionary old blimp'. Would I please tone it down?
I would not. I threw it out completely and rapidly wrote an
unusually fluent and perceptive piece about Camus, with which
to replace it.

This was our only head-on collision: and neither would budge.
Thereafter we rapidly achieved a *modus vivendi* based on (I like
to think) mutual respect, the respect of the unalike. I greatly
admire Denis Hamilton's courage and tenacity and commonsense,
his gluttony for what seems to me the most tedious kind of work,
his gift for making daring appointments, his iron nerve as he
makes his great gambling throws on the future which he seems
able to read when to me it is wholly obscure.

He is also a pleasant man to know, when you are not fighting
him; pleasant to all ranks, a real commanding officer. No one
knows the trouble he has taken to help so many colleagues who
have found themselves in need of succour. He is still a Boy Scout
at heart, like several of my best friends, and I assure you I do
not mean that as anything but a compliment. He is a middle-class
family man from the North-East of England with average tastes

but a more than average appetite for responsibility. Whatever he sets his hand to, he brings to a conclusion. You know where you stand with Denis.

When Lord Thomson bought *The Times* and Denis Hamilton was appointed Editor-in-Chief and Chief Executive of the two papers, he appointed Harold Evans as Editor of *The Sunday Times*. Harold likes to be called Harry. He too hails from the North-East, though by descent he is Welsh. He was thirty-eight when appointed; probably the youngest Editor we have had. And much the most adventurous.

He is a slight person, dark and intense-looking, handsome, with a strong jaw that speaks of determination, very eloquent blue eyes, and an apparently incurable inability to be still. He uses no drugs and is in a state of perpetual motion; I'm sure a smoke would calm him down. But I'm equally sure he doesn't particularly want to be calmed down. He likes living at top speed. And dangerously.

I am certainly not going to discuss the paper of which he is still (and doubtless will be for many years to come) the mainspring-editor. He is driving it with a furious energy along courses hitherto uncharted and unmapped. His courage is apparently boundless, his appetite for work and adventure seems insatiable. He has set his stamp on the paper with a vengeance. I find myself lost in admiration, sometimes quite out of tune. Both reactions are irrelevant: I'm not going to discuss the continuing process. The main thing is that something is definitely happening, like it or lump it. There is nothing negative or tentative about Harry's approach. It is the heroic approach. He's going to be remembered.

As a working editor he is a throwback to the old days of the working editor – immersed in the paper, digging into everything, interested in everything, fascinated by the detail. I'm sure he'd like to do every bit of it himself – write every headline and caption, plan every page, finally finish it all off on the stone in the composing room five seconds before the deadline. Of course he delegates: he has to. But here we are again with a working editor who wants to be in on everything, who is actually fascinated by the craft and its details. If it hadn't grown into such a huge organisation, I dare say he would be reading my copy and everybody else's as it was written. (He certainly reads the proofs.) But all the time that he is spending his energy on this week's issue, he is also planning ahead and imagining the paper as it will be in years to come. This is the great act of creative imagination, the thing that separates memorable editors from editors who are not remembered. Since I find myself incapable of imagining any aspect of the future without a tremor of revulsion and/or trepidation, I am lost in admiration of a man who can look steadily ahead and perceive the wayward road shaping up among the swirling mists.

Strangely enough, though he is almost young enough to be my son, I find that I can talk to Harry Evans more easily than any other editor I have worked for. That's assuming I can catch him for a talk: a tall order. There seems to be no invisible barrier, of age, class, background, style, or stance. There are none of those impalpable inhibitions, difficult to define, which have often made me unduly circumspect and diffident when trying to establish genuine human contact with some of my previous bosses. He is worried that I have so little confidence in my talent, and I am worried that he thinks I can do things which I know I am not fitted to do; but apart from that, we don't rub one another up the wrong way, we can relax and have a thoroughly uninhibited conversation – almost invariably about work, but work discussed in those highly personal terms which make it play. We lunch together occasionally, at the club or the Ivy, but we might just as well talk in the office. Harry isn't sufficiently interested in stuffing himself with food and drink to make for a relaxed meal.

I wrote once, in our house magazine of all places, that he reminded me of a Sioux chief steering the frail birchbark canoe down ghastly rapids full of razor-sharp rocks, standing up, waving his paddle, and laughing, while some members of his crew crouched below the gunwales, deep in prayer. I think it's a fairish metaphor. He certainly puts the wind up me sometimes, when my old fears surge up and I feel like a quiet life cocooned in the cosiness of the literary pages. Though no revolutionary, he is a liberal who has brought that element of calculated outrage into the paper, scaring some off, inviting some in. We may legitimately have differing views about this – some of us even have radically different views on two successive days – but history teaches us that the element of calculated outrage has been an ingredient of every paper on the way up, and absent from every paper on the

way down. I haven't always the nerve for it myself, and sometimes want to opt out and crawl into hiding, back into the womb
of the irrecoverable past. But that it is the signposted highway to
the future I have little doubt; even when I can't see the sign
posts. New readers for old – what's the exchange rate? That is
the essence of adventurous editing. It calls for a Levantine sort
of sensibility. I don't have it at all. I hope Harry does.

My refuge in this changing world, and we all need one from
time to time, is Commander J. W. Lambert, CBE, DSC. Jack
Lambert is roughly of my generation, though he has a few years
in hand of me. He has been Literary Editor of *The Sunday
Times* for many years, and has at least maintained if not improved the high standard of the literary and arts pages established
by his predecessor, my old friend Leonard Russell. A rock of
discernment and sound values, Jack is one of the very few
surviving editorial men to whom I willingly give my copy, in
the sure expectation that he will actually read it, I mean *read*
it, with distinguished attention. (Which we all think is our due.)
Jack is immensely well informed, a sagacious and penetrating
critic whose views I always listen to with respect, and withal
he is a genial companion. The hours I have spent with Jack at
the Ritz, or the Garrick, or at one of our homes, have been
among the most cheerful and stimulating. He has the generous
gift of delegating, and of choosing and encouraging good assist-
ants; he spotted the talents of Michael Ratcliffe, now the brilliant
literary editor of *The Times*, and gave them the most generous
scope; dear John Whitley has followed Michael as assistant
literary editor and perceptive reviewer of novels; and altogether
there is no place where I feel more at home, no atmosphere
more congenial, than there in the literary department of *The
Sunday Times*, a home from home and a refuge in a changing
world which alarms as often as it exhilarates me. One part of me
is avid for change, I accept the necessity for it and occasionally
I even seem to see the way ahead, dimly through the murk: but,
as often, I want the reassurance of high old standards, proof
against the erosion of neglect and triviality and the vulgar worship
of false gods: and I know where to find it.

14

At the Water

Note

I SUPPOSE I have known most of the finest fishermen of my lifetime. I know the great Richard Walker, outstanding genius of the angle, head-and-shoulders above the rest of us in sheer inventiveness, a brilliant engineer who turned his logical mind to fishing and fishing tackle and showed us all that what we thought impossible was perfectly feasible. Richard is a friend, and they don't come any more entertaining, more generous, or jollier. I'm very proud to call him a friend.

I have had the friendship of Bernard Venables for many years – a fine artist, a scholar of angling and an outstanding personality of the waterside. I know Jack Hargreaves, Fred J. Taylor, Peter Tombleson and Terry Thomas, all great men in the sport; and I have had for many years the pleasure of knowing C. V. Hancock, for so long Literary Editor and Angling Correspondent of the *Birmingham Post*, a scholarly man of letters and dedicated fly fisherman of my own West Midlands. I can call Hugh Falkus a friend, that most rare character, a devoted naturalist, a big man in every way, a heroic figure; I know and

am proud to know that I am welcome at any time at Cragg
Cottage, near Ravenglass in far Cumberland, where with his
dear wife Kathleen he presides over a lovely stretch of sea trout
and bass water – and a discerning circle of friends.

I count among my friends, though we never meet, the enthusiastic Welshman Ieuan D. Owen, one of the most fervent and
many-sided of men. It has been a joy to know the great Howard
Marshall of the golden voice, the learned entomologist David
Jacques, and many another who has proved that angling is
mysteriously more than a game, more than a sport.

I should like to celebrate them all, but this is not a fishing
book and my relations with most of them have been fishing
relations. Some of them, notably Bernard and Richard, I have
written about elsewhere, and cannot very well repeat myself.
So, therefore, though much of my leisure has been spent with
fishing friends of much distinction, as well as with some friends
of no distinction whatever, thank goodness, I have decided to
confine myself here to a couple of sketches of fellow anglers
who stay in my memory for human reasons, reasons unconnected
with angling. For it is my experience that readers who are not
interested in fishing cannot bear to read about fishing, and this
I understand.

Amos the box

AMOS was a signalman on the railway and a keen pike fisherman.
The two occupations he combined in a manner which impressed
me by its elegant economy. I formed a habit of spending some
of my afternoons, either when playing truant or when released
from school by the statutory Wednesday half-hol, in his signal
box, which was quite cosy in an austere sort of way, and
conveniently sited near the railway bridge which spanned the
canal.

This was a quiet branch line with little or no passenger traffic.
It was used mainly by coal trains shuffling to the nearby pits, and
none too many of them, in the Depression. Though I cannot say
I ever mastered the signal system, I picked up enough to be
able to relieve Amos of some of his less onerous duties. He allowed
me to swing the great gleaming levers – always with a cloth
between your sweaty hand and the polished metal, mind. After

some experience had been gained he even let me tap out messages, at his dictation, on the railway telegraph. It was marvellous to rouse up the staccato clang of the bell. But mainly my duties, such as they were, involved cleaning and stoking the fire in the stove. I was quite happy to do these jobs. It was little enough to do for the privilege of being in the box, high above the lines and the water, listening in to the man-talk of Amos and his mates, who were always dropping in for a chat. The talk was not all about fishing, by any means. It had a permanent growling sub-theme of economics, the all-pervasive economics of want and fear which gave a grey colour to that phase of life.

I chipped in one afternoon, with the feckless blithe temerity of youth. I forget what half-baked observation I made, but it stopped the conversation. Amos's friend looked at me for a minute, and noticeably looked at the grammar school cap peeping out of my pocket. Then he said something which I was never to forget:

'Yo' was born with a silver spoon in yer mouth,' he said.

I denied it hotly, but I knew that by his standards, it was true. It was a long time before I made any more contributions to the economic debate.

But when it came to fishing, I was included in, whole-heartedly, and it was here in this box that I laid the foundation of such knowledge of pike fishing as I have. Amos was an expert, and he fished for the pot, as indeed did most of the working men of the district. A fish was a meal.

Amos was a quite young man, though to me he seemed middle-aged. He had a rocky, angular face and a dead pallor, accentu-ated by a vivid blue zig-zag scar. He was married to a generously made slatternly woman with wet eyes and lips who sucked the life out of him, or so it was said. Even at the time I was vaguely aware of that. I wished to find out more about the sexual rela-tions of adults, and with the brilliant devious cunning of hunger I used to frame elaborately disguised inquiries, appearing to talk of something else but leaving the option of the *double entendre*. Several times Amos seemed on the point of confiding in me some of the knowledge with which he was, I'm sure, heavily burdened; always he bit it back at the last moment and changed the sub-ject, not adroitly, not descending to subtlety, but with a firm, blunt refusal to follow that path any longer.

There was something terribly tantalising about those experiences in the signal box, perched high over the rails and the reed-fringed, porter-coloured water, with its long round view of the plain, the pit-heads rising great and small, near and far, the great hills of spoil and slag which were our mountains, standing up sharp and crude. To a pubescent boy, riven by romance, suffused with the stirrings of sex, aflame with admiration for the ex-soldiers who were his friends, poised on the brink of a life-long love affair with poetry, edging tentatively into a new world of education and wonder and estrangement from his roots, it was a nodal point where many impulses, contradictory and congenial, seemed to fuse.

It depended on what shift Amos was working, whether he did his bit of fishing before he clocked on or after he clocked off. Sometimes there would be a small pike or jack wrapped in dock leaves keeping him company throughout the shift: once there was a brace, the object of envy and admiration. It was Amos who taught me how to gut a fish, and how to cook it. He was a better cook than his wife, the blowsy slut with the dreamily inviting eyes. In fact he taught me, without knowing it, how to cook a meal which has remained one of my favourites ever since. When we were going fishing from his home, which some-times happened, he would lay a few rashers of streaky bacon in an enamelled baking tin, with a couple of tomatoes, and put them in the oven. He trimmed off the rind and laid it over the tomatoes, to grease them. In the afternoon the little fire in the old range was banked up with slack and the oven was very slow. By the time we had done our bit of fishing it would be just nicely cooked through, and Amos would eat it out of the enamelled tin, laying it on a sheet of newspaper on the deal kitchen table, with two rounds of bread, a pot of tea and a dollop of Daddies Sauce. After watching him I would go home ravenous.

Just the other day I saw such an enamelled baking tin, identi-cal, white with a blue border, in a shop near my present home. I bought it and when I got home I laid some streaky bacon in, and two tomatoes sliced and covered with the rinds, and I put it in the oven. I ate it with white bread, tea, and a dash of Lea and Perrins fruit sauce, the nearest we had to Daddies; and the past came flooding back. But I wasn't encouraged to eat it out of the tin, which was what I really wished.

In the signal box we ate *snap*, of course, bread-and-something brought in bait cans. Some signalmen brewed tea in a big enamel teapot, but Amos used an enamelled jug, with a wire handle, the lid of which was his cup. He came to work with a stiff gob of condensed milk at the bottom of this jug, all mixed with tea and sugar. When the water which I fetched from the canal had boiled on the stove, he poured it over this speckled dollop, and stirred and stirred. A lovely fragrance came wisping up.

I begged an old frying pan, a heavy iron one, and in this, in stolen lard or dripping, we sometimes fried small roach and perch which we could catch from the canal right by the signal box. But pike were our serious quarry. We took them mainly by live-baiting, on hand lines, with slotted corks for floats. It is illegal now. It may have been illegal then. It was my pleasure and privilege to catch the live bait, which we stored in toffee tins begged from the sweet shop keepers, with a hole bodged in on opposing sides and a wire handle fixed on. Depending on the shift he was working, I would meet Amos with a supply of bait as he came on or came off duty. He was hard to please, but it saved him the time and trouble and in return for my labours I had the privileges of the signal box, the great shining levers and the telegraph key. Both sides were well satisfied with the arrangement.

I learned a lot from Amos, one way and another. When I got my first motorbike ('the silver spoon') I began to drift away. There's nothing permanent.

A college servant

I used to go fishing with a college servant whom we will call Mr Tanner. I will suppress not only his own name but the name of his college. It was not my college. I met him for the first time when I was fishing for chub in the Thames on Port Meadow.

Neither of us should have been spending our time fishing, as it turned out. I had 'better things to do', such as working to secure an affluent future either for myself (preferably) or for my fellow men. Mr Tanner should have been working on his allotment, growing vegetables for his wife and family. In fact his wife thought he *was* working on the allotment. He told me so, within five minutes of our meeting.

Mr Tanner had hooked a quite good chub which he had difficulty in landing, since he did not have a landing net. Neither did I, but I got down the bank and managed to get my fingers in the creature's gills and hauled it ashore. Mr Tanner was so grateful that he not only gave me a free choice of the luscious fat lobworms of which he had a superior selection from the allotment, writhing in moss in a tobacco tin, but he began to make me his confidant. But first he restored the chub to its freedom.

'I never keep them,' Mr Tanner said.

'Nor do I,' said I. 'You can't eat them with any pleasure.'

'Fact is I daren't take them home,' he said shyly. 'If I did she'd know I'd been fishing.'

'Who's that, your wife?'

'You might say so,' Mr Tanner said mysteriously. 'Wife in name, anyway.'

He suddenly gave me a long, severe and searching look. He was a nondescript little middle-aged man with an almost featureless face; he wore an old stained mackintosh and scarf and a black homburg hat green with age.

'You're a member of the university,' he said. It wasn't a question. I admitted it.

'Not many undergrads fish,' he said. 'You're the first I've met on the river – with a fishing rod, I mean.'

'I've always been keen on it,' I said.

'Mad keen, I am,' he said, staring at his float. 'That's why she's dead against it – because I get a bit of pleasure out of it. I'm supposed to be working on the bleeding allotment now. If she knew I was fishing she'd . . .'

'She'd *what*?' I said, as if I hadn't caught it. But he hadn't said it.

He looked at me sideways, a look of ineffable craftiness, yet somehow there was a pathos with the cunning, a haplessness which caught at the heart.

'You wouldn't understand,' he said, watching the float again.

We fished for a time in silence. He kept taking momentary looks at me, as if to gauge my suitability as a confidant. I looked as incurious as I knew how. At least I suppose I did. I tried to. But I was curious, all right.

'You want to make the most of it,' he said suddenly.

'How do you mean?'

'While you're young,' he said with passion in his voice. 'While you're free.' He reeled in and checked his bait. 'What are you going to be?'

'A journalist, I hope.'

'That's a change,' he said. 'Not many of 'em are aiming at that target. Going to be teachers, most of 'em. Or parsons.' He sniffed.

'I've had enough of teachers and teaching. I don't think I'm cut out for higher education, somehow.'

'Higher education!' he said with surprising bitterness. But perhaps it wasn't surprising, if he'd been emptying under-graduates' chamber pots all his life, and clearing up their vomit.

'You've seen a good bit of it,' I said, encouragingly.

'My good sir,' he said with grave formality, ludicrous really, 'I'll tell you where higher education starts. It starts in the bed-room.'

'Go on,' I said. He had me hooked now.

Mr Tanner pushed his homburg hat back on his head, reveal-ing a red weal across the forehead. He gave me a squinting look.

'Bitches!' He spoke as if he were spitting. 'Keep away from them, young man. Don't get hooked up. Stick to fishing.'

'Well,' I said, 'I like fishing, but....'

'I know! You want a bit of the other, as well. So did I! Dead keen I was. Keen as a ferret.' Mr Tanner's face writhed in a terrible grimace of a smile, a painful smile of self-disgust. He snapped his rod up and the tip bent to a fish. But he reeled it in peremptorily, as if the fish were a distraction.

'Tiddler,' he muttered, setting it free. He re-baited with a lob-worm as big as a small grass snake and hurled it out into the flow. 'That'll scare the tiddlers off.' He re-adjusted his hat. 'They eat you alive,' he said.

'Who do?' But I knew what he meant.

'Women,' said Mr Tanner. 'Women.'

He glared at his float.

'Can't call your soul your own,' said Mr Tanner. He was muttering to himself now. 'Yes, dear. No, dear. Three bags full, dear.' Then he seemed to recollect my presence. 'If I could have my time again, you know what I'd do?'

'No, what?'

'I'd be off like a shot. I would an' all. On the ships. I could've had a berth, once, on one of them cruise liners. What a life, eh?

Talk about higher education! In and out of foreign ports, live like a lord, love 'em and leave 'em. . . .' Mr Tanner bared his teeth in a soundless cackle. 'Love 'em and leave 'em,' he said again, rolling it round his tongue. 'That's the ticket. Especially leave 'em.'

'That's your advice, is it?'

'Never doubt it,' said Mr Tanner. *'Never ... doubt ... it.'* He dug into his clothing and produced a battered silver watch. 'Jesus College! I'll have to be denying myself the pleasure of your company. I'd no idea it was that time. Christ Church almighty! If I don't get round to the allotment and pull a few leeks she'll have my guts for garters. See you again, young sir, I hope.'

I did indeed see Mr Tanner again, on several occasions. At first I sought him out, but eventually he drove me away from the river. The half-promised revelations never came. His first conversation was endlessly repeated, and after a time the lugubrious and bitter reiteration of alleged tyranny, unsubstantiated by juicy detail though obviously all too true, began to pall. I took to avoiding Mr Tanner.

He was a very good fisherman, I may say.

Will

I met Will, and his darling wife Nellie, at the George Hotel in Hatherleigh, Devon. We were having a fishing holiday. There are few more productive places in which to find congenial friends than a good fishing hotel.

The George was a good fishing hotel. They had a few nice beats on the Torridge, where the brown trout ran very small but the sea trout ran large and the salmon were satisfactory. By which I mean you had to work for them. I've never been rich enough to have a rod on one of those fabled beats where you can expect half a dozen salmon a day, but I'm perfectly happy if there are *some* fish running in the river, enough to persuade you that you're not wasting your time, but not enough to make it too easy. The George also had water on the Lew and the Okement, known locally as the Okkey, where it was really more or less trouting only, and very nice too.

But never mind the fishing, the George was a really nice

place to stay, very old and interesting architecturally, with a lovely upstairs sitting room all chintzy and knick-knackery, where you could relax all evening after dinner, with a pot of coffee or even tea, and mull it all over. The food was superb. There was a local lass named Ruby, a dream girl, who was perfectly willing to come in and cook you a huge steak supper if you wanted to stay out fishing late.

I had spotted this 1926 Rolls-Royce in the stable before we went in. It was a Park Ward convertible which had been quite cleverly cut down, a real collector's item. When Will heard us talking at breakfast and made himself known (he had read some of my stuff) I didn't need telling that he was the Rolls-Royce owner. It couldn't have been anyone else. He had the look for it. I don't mean rolling rich, not that sort of Rolls-Royce man; just interesting, characterful, and distinguished.

When I saw his rod this impression was confirmed. He was there for the trout, not the salmon, and he used a greenheart fly rod made by Hardy's at about the same time that Rolls-Royce made the car, and just as elegant and distinguished and dated.

The same was true of his tweed suit, his briar pipe and flake, his hair style and his conversation. Will was an original, a man of distinctive style and perception, of excellent taste and quite without a trace of subservience to the ordinances of the mass media.

When we fell to talking, that night in the chintzy upstairs sitting room in which Jane Austen would have felt at home, I knew that I had found a rare one.

Will Nickless is quite possibly the most remarkable and almost certainly the most versatile man of my acquaintance. As I have come to know him better, over the years, my admiration of his many-sidedness has increased. He may not be the most success-ful fly fisherman of my acquaintance, but he is certainly the most distinctive. For he is so much more.

By profession and vocation, Will is an artist. His oil paintings are distinguished by their technical virtuosity – and romanticism. He has earned his living, mainly, as an illustrator. He began, I think, as a technical draughtsman on *The Motor* – the older generation of aficionados will recall with nostalgic admiration his superb sectional working drawings. But his range is wide, his catholicity considerable. He drew for *Radio Times* for many years. He has done strip cartoons and a great variety of book illustrations (he embellished a number of my own books). There is virtually nothing he cannot accomplish with a high degree of apparently effortless professional skill – and individual distinction.

But when you come to know him as a friend, you realise that the accomplishment of his hands and mind are altogether exceptional and outside the normal categories. For instance, he has made a working telescope with his own hands – and that included grinding the lenses himself, from the raw glass. He can make violins, cellos, flutes. His miniature railway, any boy's delight, is a miracle of verisimilitude and conviction – and he built it with his own hands from the raw metal, perfect to the smallest detail.

He has owned only three cars in his longish life, but what a trio. The first was a three-litre Bentley, the Van den Plas open tourer, the Red Label model of historic memory. The second was the Rolls-Royce Park Ward convertible two-seater. The third is a beautiful Freestone & Webb Continental touring coupé on the Rolls-Royce 25 h.p. chassis. He maintains his cars himself, going so far as to rebore the engines when necessary, and reline the brakes.

You don't have to be rich to enjoy the best – *if* you have Will's aptitudes and patience and profound skills. You *do* have to have the innate and cultivated taste which recognises the best.

Will is a perfectionist, I suppose. When I think of Will I think of something which Dr James Williams wrote about his own father, in his very enjoyable little book, *Give Me Yesterday*. Describing those far-off winter evenings in the little farmhouse in West Wales where he was brought up, Dr Williams tells us how they sat around the ingle, toasting bits of home-made cheese and whittling away at sycamore baulks to make the 'treen' which the household used – plates, spoons, ladles and so on; and the besoms and axe handles and all the rest of the lovely stuff. Of his father he says:

'He supervised our work and quietly, without fuss, demonstrated the skills involved in making each article well. The second-rate was completely unacceptable to him – he had one aim only, to achieve perfection in big or small tasks. His mansuetude was boundless; but it did not permit him to accept the second-rate.'

When I read that I thought of dear old Will. It fits him to a t.

Will is originally a Londoner, and when we came to know him and Nellie they were still living in St John's Wood. But for many years now they have lived in a remarkably and deeply romantic house in Sussex, secluded by its belt of tall and ancient trees, standing on the edge of a village and bounded by tranquil farmland. We never visited that gracious house without a deep feeling that we were going back in time, back to an era before electronics and mass media and mass propaganda. There has never been a television set in the house; indeed, the sound of the radio has never been heard therein. Will takes *The Times*, and that is all. He and Nellie do everything for themselves; life goes forward tranquilly, quietly, with work and reading, music, sewing, writing, gardening. Will has written several books, including that exceptional work of imagination, the series 'for children' which began with *Owlglass* and continued through *The Nitehood*, *Molepie*, and *Dotted Lines*. He is a pacifist, a close and profound student of oriental philosophy and comparative religion. He is a perfect example of a man who is his own man, who is eclectic and discriminating. He has chosen his way, among the many, and followed it with quiet resolution.

It has always been fine to visit there, that quiet old house full of pictures, full of books, full of artefacts largely created by Will himself. Hours we have spent in the big work-room or study – so much more than a study, more even than a studio – with the elegant old-fashioned rods in their glass-fronted case, alongside the dully-gleaming good guns; the tools and the documents, the tools of several trades, the instruments of several obsessions. Always you felt you were in the presence of a rare spirit, a Renaissance man, a man so multiplex and various, yet so unified and at peace.

Captain Blood

I was fishing the upper reaches of a Welsh Border stream, fishing with the fly, for trout or grayling or whatever it might contain. It was a lonely country and I had fished down two miles of the stream when I saw that figure awaiting me, leaning on the old stone bridge. There was not a building in sight, there was nothing but mountain and moorland and the chuckling stream, nothing but sheep and high drifting clouds, high drifting birds of prey, and memories of battles long ago.

He leaned upon the parapet as if he too were cut from the same rough stone; stone of the mountains, flesh of the everlasting hills. He never stirred. He wore a deerstalker hat and a Norfolk jacket with pleats, and knickerbockers, though those were hidden from my view as I approached. His face was craggy and weather-beaten, he had a huge purplish nose, his eyebrows bristled. I raised a hand in salutation and he raised a hand in reply. But he went on waiting, watching every cast. It is not easy to keep your composure when someone leaning over the parapet of a bridge is watching your every cast, with such gravity and attention. When I was within half a dozen casts of him I reeled in and walked up to the bridge and greeted him civilly.

'You fish downstream,' he said.

'Sometimes.'

'I fish upstream.'

'Invariably?'

'Invariably.'

'It takes all sorts,' I said, fishing out my tobacco pouch. He darted me a fierce glance. His eyes were flecked with blood, the whites yellow, flecked with red. Associating his nose, which was flecked with tiny blue veins, with his eyes which were flecked with red, I drew certain conclusions. Perhaps uncharitably.

'Think so?' he said. 'You believe that?'

'It's self-evident.'

'That's a defeatist view, sir.'

I smiled at the old boy. He was off his rocker, I thought. You meet some odd ones.

'We're not all cut from the same cloth,' I ventured.

'No, by gad! You're right there. We're *not* all cut from the same cloth. That's precisely the point I'm making.'

' 'Fraid I don't follow you. I'm making the point that it's all diversity. You said that was defeatism. Now you say you agree with me.'

'Don't you see, m'boy, some of us are qualified to set the standard – just because we are cut from finer cloth than the lumpen proletariat? Don't you feel any *responsibility*?'

'I'm all responsibility,' I said warmly. 'I get so damn sick of responsibility that I come fishing, occasionally. Glad to get away from it.'

'But you can't get away from it,' the old boy said. 'Look here, you're British, I take it?'

'To the core.'

'And you're one of us – you're not a bloody yobbo, I can tell that. Dare say you've served your country?'

'I was in the war.'

'And I was in the other one – the *real* war. Captain in the Gunners. Knocked about a bit. I never thought I'd see this country what it is today. Bolshies, yobboes, wogs ... Know what I put it down to?'

'I'd be interested to hear.' May I be forgiven.

'*Standards,*' the captain said, looking me in the eye. 'No moral fibre, no leadership, people damn well afraid to stand up and be counted. Too much damn toleration – leads to laxity. Now take your case –'

'*My* case?'

'I believe in giving it straight. You were fishing the wet fly, weren't you? Downstream?'

'Yes. The March Brown, silver-bodied. What of it?'

'It's the principle of the thing. Always fish the dry fly myself. Always. Upstream and the dry fly.'

'Good for you. I often do myself. But there's no hatch – no fish rising. Makes sense to fish the sunk fly when no fish are showing. And I was coming back downstream anyway. It makes sense to vary your tactics to suit the situation.'

Captain Blood laid a hand on my shoulder.

'My dear boy, you've put it in a nutshell. You change your approach to suit the situation. Don't you see where that leads?'

'Frankly, no.'

'It leads to maggot slinging,' the captain said with passion. 'It leads to *spinning*. It leads to poaching. Once you abandon the principle of the upstream dry fly, thrown to rising fish, you're on the way to netting. You're on your way to cyanide. You might as well chuck a grenade in the damn water and have done with it.'

I had to laugh.

'You may laugh, my young friend. I've seen this country change – and change for the worse! – ah, damnably – and all because people let themselves slide. It begins with little things, it ends up in –'

'Miscegenation?'

Captain Blood turned and gazed into my eyes. He was silent for a minute. When he spoke his voice was sad and low.

'Precisely. It ends with miscegenation. It ends in moral anarchy. It begins with letting standards slip, letting things slide ... people who ought to show leadership indulge themselves, the yobboes rush in to follow ... it ends up with nobody giving a tuppenny damn for anything. Don't you see the sequence? Don't you see it's all a matter of breeding and leadership, moral courage?'

Years of misuse had made that vibrant gravelly voice. I said:

'Actually I've got a lot of sympathy with that élitist point of view. But I don't take it to such extremes. I'm quite severe on myself.... I never fish for trout with anything more reprehensible than the fly, as a matter of fact. I'm rather stuffy about standards of behaviour, I'm an absolute pedant when it comes to spelling and syntax.... But I'm afraid I don't see myself as divinely ordained to give a lead to others who are entitled to different views.'

'Sad,' said the captain. 'No one takes it seriously now. But I know it's right. Leadership, my boy. That's what we were selected by Destiny to give. It's in the blood. Or it *was*. Everything's going to pot. Bolshie rabble-rousers ... spivs ... bloody darkies ... Jack's as good as his master ... no pride in craftsmanship ... where'll it all end?'

'A lot of people are better-off than ever they were before,' I ventured.

'H'm. You a bolshie, m'boy?'

'Hardly. I'm an old-style pre-war liberal, I suppose. I get a bit more conservative all the time. I actually believe in conserving the things we both want conserved, you and I. But I like to see the cake shared out a bit more generously. I like a bit of social flux. I'm afraid I don't share your views about the divine mission of the blood.'

'Know what I am?' the captain asked. 'I'm a bloody reactionary. And I'm proud of it. They'll let you down, my boy. They'll spoil it all. Got to stick to what you believe in. Straight bat, upstream only, fish the rise, keep the wogs and yobboes in their place. They were better off when they knew their place. I make no bones about it. Wishy-washy bloody liberals parading their delicate consciences. Makes me sick. *I* don't feel guilty, me boy. Damned if I do.'

I grinned at the old boy. Couldn't help it. 'There aren't many left like you, captain.'

'Damn few, you know. And soon there won't be any. I bid you good day, sir.'

And he stalked off down the lane. And a hawk flew high.

Argon

ARGON was a prince of China who served as a diplomat in London, under the régime of the Nationalist leader Chiang Kai-shek, during the ambassadorship of the successor to the great Doctor Wellington Koo. It was the last, the final embassy of Nationalist China before Mao Tse Tung won his victory. Needless to say, we were not aware of this finality, at the time when we became friendly with Argon. We believed that it was the beginning of a lifelong friendship.

I am sure that it would have been so, had not the unimaginable tide of history swept it away like a sand castle.

The chosen name Argon signifies Light. It was the name by which his friends called him. It was well chosen. He was a young, slight and gay man, with a light touch, and he seemed to radiate light. The lightness emanated from a fundamental seriousness; we were put in mind of those revealing pictures of a total eclipse, when the nimbus of light glares and dances all round the dark hot core.

Argon lived next door to us in Chesterford Gardens, Hampstead – just off Frognal, on the way up towards the Heath. He had a flat between the house in which we had the mezzanine flat, with dear Vicky and Mary Lees in the garden flat below, and the house occupied by other friends, Sir Geoffrey and Lady Cox. It was that curious period, soon after the end of the Second World War, when we were trying out the feel of London life, tasting it, wondering if we might settle down as Hampstead professional people – I was an executive in Fleet Street at the time – or bolt for the country and the writing life. We bolted, but not before we had savoured the peculiar pleasures of that sort of life. And one of the keenest of those pleasures, which were many and various, was the friendship of Argon.

I was supposed to be helping him to polish up his English. In fact he understood it and spoke it well, as he understood French quite well. He had been stationed in Paris and in Washington before coming to London. But he was tremendously keen that his English should be idiomatic as well as correct, and we formed a habit of holding practice sessions, almost invariably over tea or dinner, occasionally luncheon. Argon also telephoned me every day, to read out fragments from *The Times* which struck him as difficult or entertaining – especially fragments from the classified advertisements. Occasionally I found myself not knowing the required answer.... Argon's voice when talking to you face to face was soft and gentle, but like others he had an exaggerated scepticism of the telephone and tended to shout into it, as if by shouting he could overcome the instrument's in-built deficiencies. From this it followed that my wife also took part in our telephone conversations. As often as not they ended with a suggestion that he might as well save his breath, and money, and come round for a cup of tea or a drink.

O, those exquisite little tea parties *à trois*, when we learned how to make and dispense tea in the appropriate manner, and learned, too, a little of how it felt to be ten thousand miles from home, a lodger in an alien civilisation which not even the most fervently patriotic could assume superior at every point.... We gradually learned that Argon's father was or had been a wealthy mandarin and that he, the only son, had spent most of his life in learning, learning. He was wonderfully well informed, his mind was alive and alert, he was insatiably curious, avid for more knowledge. Yet withal he was the gentlest and simplest of beings, never censorious, invariably courteous and kind and gay. He was heavenly company.

Looking back now, I realise how rich that period of Hampstead living was, rich in the experience of cosmopolitan good company – and distinguished company, which are not invariably the same thing. During this period we were visited by friends from France, we had delightful Hungarian friends next door, we had Greek friends and Indian friends, Spanish friends and Turkish friends, Armenian and Danish friends, Arab and Israeli friends. None perhaps especially close, none so intimate as Argon; but there was a coming and going, an intermingling, which was good for us and which I now realise I miss in our more sequestered life, though that has other attractions.

It is quite hard to remember how straitened life was in Britain in the late 'Forties and early 'Fifties. Rationing was still in force, sometimes more stringent than during the war: the meat ration went down to a shilling's-worth a week, there was even talk of bread rationing, which had never been suggested during the war; sweets were rationed, petrol short, a new car was for most people impossible to come by – you had to wait anything up to three years, and then a covenant was slapped on to prevent you from re-selling it at a big profit. Life thawed out gradually, but Crippsian austerity was all the rage in politics, spivvery was rampant elsewhere, and, as usual, it was the rich wot got the pleasure, the poor wot got the blame. The cold snap of 1947 found us without fuel; the BBC had to close down for considerable periods, to save electricity, and the ordinary citizen had to put up with endless power cuts. It seemed by no means a land fit for heroes; whatever one may think of the socialist ideals which led our rulers to impose this needless austerity in the name of equal suffering, it was a first-rate mess purely from the point of view of efficient administration, and human nature did not look too lovely.

Things were just beginning to look a little less dour when we became friendly with Argon, and he used the advantages of his diplomatic position to make life nicer for his friends. He obtained a brand-new car, an Austin A40, the slightly egg-shaped 1200c.c. car which inaugurated that long line; he had all the petrol he could use; he ate well at the embassy and had ration cards for food for home consumption such as we only dreamed of. Not to mention an apparently inexhaustible supply of drink. Neither of us will ever forget those small dinner parties in Argon's flat, when he taught us the rudiments of Chinese cooking – *low-oil-quick-stir-fry*, to translate literally. Argon would have the food laid out on the kitchen table when we arrived. Typically, a pound or so of succulent steak, half pound of precious lard, tomatoes, leeks, rice, noodles and so on. We would cook the meal while wandering around, glass in hand; each contributing his mite of work. It was a great sight to see Argon throwing wet leeks into boiling fat from a distance of six feet.

He was still uncertain about some Western terms. On our arrival, the first time, he pressed whisky and gin upon us, the standard hard liquor of the Western world, its principal anodyne. I was nothing loth, needless to say, though even I blanched (or blushed) to receive a tumberful of the stuff undiluted and unashamed. Kay shied off like a frightened filly and asked in a small voice if she might have a soft drink, instead.

'Soft drink? Certainly!' Argon cried happily. We naturally assumed that he knew what he was talking about. He went to the sideboard and withdrew a bottle of port, which he proceeded to glug-glug into a tumbler, quite a big tumbler. When Kay faintly protested he was not at all put out. He poured her a tumblerful of Green Chartreuse instead.

If we were able to put a few touches of polish on Argon's education in Western ways, details like the composition of soft drinks and the idiom of *Times* leaders and letters and small ads, it was nothing compared with what he taught us. He was our first Chinese friend, our first friend rooted in Asia, the continent which has always drawn my imagination. I know Europe fairly well, though my knowledge is rapidly becoming rusty, but I have never been farther afield. I never particularly fancied Africa, or the Antipodes, or the Indian sub-continent; but I always longed to see China. Not the China of the war-lords, but the China of the scholars and ancestor-worshippers; China of the mandarin and the peasant, China of the family and the land, China where art had frozen and custom had congealed, China where the way to office lay through scholarship, China where the vegetable was treated with reverence, China of gamblers and poets, China that had disdained to exploit its discovery of gunpowder for anything more lethal than fireworks, China where printing was an old story, China that disdained the barbarians with their engines.

It is too late now. I do not wish to visit the China that has stooped to the level of the barbarians, the new China where the past is no longer respected and the rude engines are being copied. I do not wish to see a people living under the dictatorship of the least civilised, slaves from childhood to the cruel propaganda of hate.

Argon wished to know more of the West, I dearly wished to know more of China; it was pure curiosity, propaganda never entered into the deal, as we spent the hours, by day and by night, at our flat and at his, walking the streets, driving in his new little car to Brighton and back, eating the exiguous meals which restaurants could offer or the simple feasts which we contrived from his rations for ourselves. Or simply taking the tea ceremony, of all the dearest, the simplest and yet most charged with a civilised significance.

It was a friendship that lasted about two years, until the news came, quite incredible, that the Communists had won, had driven the government which employed him out of the mainland and into Taiwan, Formosa. Argon remained perfectly composed. He was a liberal through and through, in the finest sense of that holy word; at the end we were not certain whether he would go to Formosa, or to the mainland. He was impervious to ideology. He was a beautiful soul, generous and gentle, brave and gay. When he said goodbye it was we who were in tears. We received a postcard from him, posted en route at Singapore; then silence fell. I think of him sometimes when the sun rises on our little plot and

Night falls on China, the great arc of travelling shadow ...

16

Squire

THERE have been two squires in my life, Squire Vernon of Hatherton and Squire Harry Stuart Goodhart-Rendel of Hatchlands, East Clandon. I really can hardly claim the acquaintance of Squire Vernon. He ruled mysteriously on the far edge of the known world when I was a boy. Where the 'free' known country of farmland and industry and pits ended, his shrouded estate began, closely fenced, keepered, exclusive, aloof, belonging to a different world; feudal, despotic, a landed-gentry way of life quite alien to our world of work and wages. I entered his territories, uninvited, poached small game, bivouacked in the undergrowth, once set his bracken on fire, for a dare. Luckily it failed to spread.

Squire Vernon was more geographical than human, as a figure in our lives. Squire Vernon's Hill was our local test gradient, said to be one-in-six, though more likely one-in-eight. A motorbike that could climb Squire Vernon's was a good 'un – these were days of single-speed or 'variable pulley' belt drives. A cyclist who could dash down Squire Vernon's with his feet on the handlebars was also a good 'un. Many failed to negotiate the sharp left-hander at the foot of the hill; my own parents, and my wife's parents, in their courting days, cycling down Squire Vernon's came to grief and ended in the steep bank below the hedgerow, sweet-smelling bank of wayside flowers.

A little beyond the foot of Squire Vernon's Hill was a rivulet known to us as The Little Brook, which meandered out of the Squire's formidably fenced demesne, and crossed underneath the lane through a cast-iron pipe just big enough for a venturesome man to crawl through – my Uncle Simpson made family history by proving that this could be done, with his shoes and socks off and his black trousers rolled up, and him a parson. The real country, for us, began at this point, where Squire Vernon's Hill precipitated us down from the windy high plateau into the gentle maze of lanes and farms that led through Shareshill to Four Ashes, Gailey, Brewood, Shifnal, Weston-under-Lizard, Albrighton and Tong. There was some nice quiet country in Staffordshire then; I dare say there is today, but it's a long time since I saw it.

But Squire Vernon was merely a remote feudal figure, archaic and anachronistic, whom we ordinary working people of the industrial part never met, never even saw, most of us, and owed no allegiance to. Actually, as I have since learned, he was a benign and charming old autocrat living his own life out in the way he knew, immersed in the immemorial pursuits of the landed gentry. He did not impinge on our lives at all, he was simply a familiar name given to familiar places. It was thirty years later when I met the second squire in my life, and his direct personal influence was prodigiously more potent.

When Kay and I decided that we were not cut out for the high life in Hampstead, we began to search the small ads in *The Times* and *The Sunday Times*, with unremitting assiduity, looking for a country cottage which we might rent. Rent, of course; we had no capital, and no prospect of ever having any. After a year or so we spotted one for an '*Elizabethan Cottage*', in East Clandon, Surrey. I instantly took the day off, it was Friday I remember, and we pottered off down there in our new acquisition, one of the reasons why we saw no prospect of ever owning capital, a clapped-out A.C. two-seater convertible, vintage 1933.

In this beautiful and feline car, painted that lustrous deep midnight blue which A.C.s always did so well, we found our way to East Clandon and the cottage, which was temporarily tenanted by Rudd Jones, farm manager at Old Manor Farm which by a curious chance was inhabited by the estate agent who was also the agent for the estate (you're with me?) and his wife Jean. Rudd and Jean fetched us up short by mentioning casually that scores or at least dozens of couples had reached it before us; in fact 266 people made application for that jolly old heap, which was offered at £150 a year on a seven-year lease.

When we went into Guildford to see the agent, Paul Luxmoore May, he gave us a delightful surprise by asking if we would be prepared to be interviewed by the squire. I didn't think there were any squires left – this was 1950 – but of course I said yes, we'd be glad to be surveyed and even grilled by the old man. It was a very attractive cottage and a very low rent. Luxmoore warned us, very nicely I thought, that the squire was none too keen to open up the village at all, to strangers – this was the very first of the old cottages which had been 'modernised' (somewhat sketchily) and offered to all comers at what was presumably thought to be an economic rent. The squire, it turned out, was far from keen on having gin-swilling cocktail-party types coming into the village, and adamant that it should not be let to week-enders; he wanted it lived in by people who were prepared to become full-time members of the community.

Well, we filled the bill, or so it seemed. The very last thing we wanted was a weekend cottage; we were for putting down roots again. And as for cocktail parties and all that, why were we leaving Hampstead and the intellectual-professional circus? So we passed scrutiny – the factor that finally tipped the scales was my occupation as a writer on *The Sunday Times*, which older readers will recall was a very respectable newspaper. So we moved in.

It took time for it to sink in that East Clandon under squire's aegis was still an almost feudal village. Not quite, of course; the hairline cracks in the dam were just visible, modernity was seeping in: there were four cars and one television receiver. But by and large it was a village where time had stood still. Squire lived still in the great house, Hatchlands, and though he didn't own the entire village he owned so much of it that his word was virtually law. I had thought our 'economic rent' very economical indeed at £150 p.a., but when I realised that most of the cottages were let at rents of the order of 1s 6d (7½ new pence) a week, some actually free, some half-a-crown (12½p), and so on, I began to see the light.

Harry Stuart Goodhart-Rendel held the Hatchlands estate (which virtually meant the village) in trust. I can't just recall what his relationship was to the late Lord Rendel, who was still remembered in the village, and it doesn't matter. He was a bachelor who lived alone in the great house, served by a butler and various other retainers. Among his distinguished friends he numbered the Princess Royal and John Betjeman, who wandered into Rudd Jones's cottage one Sunday morning (Rudd had moved to the cowman's cottage) asking plaintively if they had a fixture into which he might plug his electric razor, since he couldn't find one at Hatchlands. He said he fancied their breakfast too.

I imagine there is no doubt whatsoever that Harry Stuart Goodhart-Rendel was the only man who both held the Slade Professorship of Fine Arts *and* wrote a drill manual for the Brigade of Guards. The dual distinction perhaps indicates something of the quality of this exceptional, distinguished and most unusual man. He was an only child, an architect by profession, and a Grenadier. Some of the villagers still referred to him as Captain, or the Captain – just as, I discovered later, villagers in Wiltshire referred to their local squire, Siegfried Sassoon, as the Captain. Once a year in midsummer squire had the band of the Grenadier Guards down for the day; they played and marched on the lawn of Hatchlands, watched by the tenantry and by squire's special guests, then tucked in to a splendid tea before departing for Caterham or wherever it may have been.

But that was not by any means the only old-time idiosyncrasy. Every Christmas time, before departing at year's end to his house in southern France (he suffered from asthma and needed to escape the rigours of the English winter), squire gave a children's tea party at Hatchlands, complete with conjuror and Christmas tree, oranges and gifts for all comers. We attended his celebration for several years running, scarcely able to believe that it was happening: the butler, the children's tea separate from the adult guests' tea, the entertainment, the present-giving, the perfunctory but official speeches, the wonderfully English mixing of diverse guests on a basis of limited social licence.

Squire was an exceptionally cultivated man who had few illusions about the nature of his relationship with the tenantry. He told me that he was quite aware that the sporting farmers could not understand him because he had no time for country sports. He did not hunt, shoot, or fish. His passions were music, art, a rather eclectic choice of literature, the Grenadiers, and the Roman Catholic church. He attended a Catholic chapel in the neighbouring village of Horsley – I rather fancy he had built it, though there I cannot be quite certain. But it would be probable: he built quite a few. Ecclesiastical architecture was his speciality and passion: he had a close association with the monks of Prinknash Abbey in Gloucestershire, where he was eventually buried. His faith led him to a remarkable view of history, at any rate English history, which, I sometimes suspected, ended for him with the battle of Bosworth Field. All that had happened since was an aberration in his eyes. He could not refer to the Tudors without emotion. He invariably referred to Queen Elizabeth the Virgin as 'Anne Boleyn's child'. He used to spit it out: 'Anne *Bullen's* child.' The Reformation was something that had happened yesterday; having known him, I am better able to understand how to some twentieth-century people the Battle of the Boyne is also something that happened yesterday.

Needless to say, squire was deeply conservative, permeated with an intense antipathy to change. He was personally one of the kindest, as one of the most upright and charitable, of men. But I fear he saw no virtue in the developments towards democracy (such as they were) that had taken place since 1485. He did not go about expressing reactionary sentiments; propaganda was nothing to him; he simply lived *as if* change might be not merely resisted, but ignored.

He had living with him, for some years after we became his tenants, his old stepfather Wilbraham Cooper, a man so steeped in feudalism that when it was proposed that bathrooms and modern sanitation should be installed in some of the cottages, he observed, 'Do the peasants really want bathrooms?' This, after the Second World War. Squire would not have gone so far; he was humane and he was also an architect; he wanted his tenants to have indoor privies and bathrooms, running water and electric light. But I think he also wanted them to live in peace in a socially and aesthetically changeless environment.

Who can lay his hand on his heart and asseverate that they are *happier* now that the flood-tide of change has swept through that enchanted village where time, even so recently as 1955, seemed to be standing still?

We were for a long time, several years, the only strangers to intrude; the village consisted of three independent farmers with their satellites, and an Anglican (bachelor) rector, a hearty chaplain figure who boasted of having served in all three Services, and squire and his household, and an extraordinary assortment of outworkers known as the estate staff, who looked after not only the big house, park, and gardens, but all the dependent cottages. There were two woodmen or foresters, a carpenter and mate, a couple of decorators, and Frank and Tim who did the brickwork and all other work. We enjoyed the services of these stalwarts, on a happy-go-lucky basis, a number of times, though ours was supposed to be a repairing lease, and became close friends with one of them, Tim, who had been squire's batman in the Grenadiers and had followed him to Clandon. Tim and Frank came to clean the chimney, unblock drains, and do odd jobs that wanted doing: it was all very much on a 'we'll be seeing you', 'just slipped over', cup-of-tea-and-wad basis. It was barely credible, but thoroughly enjoyable.

We were quite willing, when we had a bob to spare, to improve the old cottage, but squire was extremely resistant to improvements. He was always walking round the village, when in residence, keeping a sharp eye open for unofficial change. All the tenants' cottages were uniformly painted in repellent colours, dark drab browns and greens – because they always *had* been. Our lease was generous and amiable enough about actual money, but extremely particular about paint: we were not free to vary the textures and finishes by a shade. (Our paint, thank goodness, was white.) One day we set to and knocked out a sizeable piece of inner wall in order to build a recessed or flush bookcase alongside the ingle. It was barely complete when squire called to have a cup of tea and listen to some Alfred Deller records that we thought highly of. He stared menacingly at the improvement throughout the music, and was plainly on the brink of uttering. Fortunately the sound of that distinguished counter-tenor pleased him so much that he thought better of it. But you could see he was shaken by our temerity.

We were invited to meals at the great house occasionally, but I'm afraid they were not the most relaxed of social occasions. I shall remember our first luncheon. In the vast lofty dining room, Wilbraham was served alone at a small table, while we shared a round table with squire. It was more like eating at a restaurant or club than at a private house. We were a little put out by this antique figure champing away just behind us, not taking part in the general conversation but interjecting a wholly unintelligible remark now and again when the stunning pictures on the walls were being discussed. It called for more social *savoir faire* than I possessed to cope with this gnomic apparition muttering away just behind my left shoulder. The food was delicious, but the drink was peculiar. Kay and I were given champagne, but squire had a small decanter of whiskey and soda, ready mixed, which which he supported what was certainly a fairly difficult conversation.

But he was a dear old boy, we became very fond of him, and I think he had a soft spot for us. He used to come and tell us of his troubles – everyone has them – and forecast the havoc that would fall upon the village when he was dead. The estate was to pass from his care into the hands of two relatives, a split that he regarded with misgivings. Sure enough, the village has now been sold to various bidders, at remarkable prices, the old cottages have been tarted up and few if any of the original inhabitants, I mean the 1950 natives, remain. It's interesting to recall that our cottage has just changed hands (last year, 1971) for £18,250. It was offered to me in 1961 for £7,500, after squire's death. I refused to pay what I thought was an extortionate price, and we left the village. Wrong again.

You always knew when squire was making his rounds. 'Dogs! Dogs!' he would cry, in a real Grenadier's voice. The dogs ran ahead – they wouldn't survive five minutes with today's traffic – and at length that tall, spare, upright figure hove into view, marching along, twirling his stick, looking in his grey tweed suit and soft brown trilby remarkably like that other Grenadier, Harold Macmillan, except that his moustache took a downward turn. He would pause and pass the time of day, perhaps come in and inspect the garden, in which he thought Kay had done well, as she had, and leave me with a crisp comment on Belloc, or *The Times*, or indeed the times; none of which in his opinion were what they had been. Evelyn Waugh would have been fascinated by him.

I suppose the whole squire régime lasted about ten years, so far as we were concerned; but it was like a little lifetime, that decade; an interlude of stability and apparent changelessness, while we were growing into middle-age. The great house is a girls' school now, a finishing school as I understand it, and by a pleasing irony which would have appealed to squire's mordant sense of the inadvisability of change, there is a sort of Borstal institution down the lane, just past keeper's cottage by the little lake where the carp and the mallard colony throve.

Sometimes when we think back to the years with squire in the big house we find it not altogether easy to believe that things were really as we remember them. But they were. I don't know how many villages in England survived under the squirearchy so late into the twentieth century. It cannot have been very many. I doubt very much if there are many figures alive today like that strange, good, kind, conservative man. In the ideological sense, he 'stood for' a number of things to which I was intellectually and even emotionally opposed. But ideologies are limiting things. He had to go, he had to be the last of his race; he could no more dam the tide of change than could Canute. Society had changed, almost radically, almost without his noticing: though he had his suspicions, he feared the future. None of this prevented him from being a compassionate gentleman who did his paternal duty, as he saw it, to people who did not always understand or appreciate him. I salute his memory.

17

Siegfried

My life has been suffused with poetry, but I have known few poets. I have met W. II. Auden once, in the Green Room of the Birmingham Rep.; Louis MacNeice once, fleetingly, also in Birmingham; Dylan Thomas once. The only eminent poet with whom I have had anything to call a conversation was Siegfried Sassoon. Poets are shy, and so am I.

I had read every word that he had published, but the opportunity of meeting Siegfried Sassoon did not come until he was in the last decade of his long life. Jack Lambert gave me an exquisite book of his poems called *The Path to Peace*, beautifully printed by the nuns of Stanbrook Abbey, Worcester. It contained only twenty-eight poems, written between 1909 and 1960, selected by the Abbess of Stanbrook to commemorate and elucidate the old huntsman's lifelong gallop over the heavy clay lands of doubt, the monstrous fences of scepticism, in pursuit of the faith which he found at last in the seventy-first year of his age.

It struck me that I might usefully seek an interview with the poet, to discuss the winding path that had led him from heroic rebellion during the Great War to the peace of the Roman

Catholic Church. With Jack's approval I went ahead, and one dowly day in a cold Spring I found myself driving in to the village of Heytesbury in Wiltshire, where I was directed to 'Captain Sassoon's place' by a village woman who took an obvious pride in the place's reluctant and retiring celebrity. It was the great house of the village, a splendid mansion set in its park. But the lodge was untenanted, and when I reached the house I found that the total domestic 'staff' was a charming and doughty young woman who had come in to do some work and get the Captain's tea (and mine) and who seemed to be, indeed was, the only help he had.

When Siegfried entered the beautiful high room in which I had been put to wait, thin as a rake, looking ten years younger than his age, it was a toss-up which of us was the shyer, the less at ease. But his courtesy was exquisite, and within a quarter of an hour or so, when presumably he discovered that I wanted to talk or rather hear him talk about his work, he unfroze and became delightfully genial and forthcoming and at ease. And so did I. (After the article had appeared he wrote me a charming letter, unfortunately lost, telling me that he was satisfied that I hadn't sensationalised or misrepresented him. I was very proud of that. A journalist should always be able to go back. But not all may.)

Before tea, and over tea, he talked to me about his war-time experiences, when he was both hero and rebel. It was the white-hot poetry of protest which was lit in his sensitive soul by the horrors and protraction and what he took to be the political misdirection of the Great War that made him famous overnight. A modern generation much more accustomed to protest would approve this side of him: but it has also to be remembered that before he was a protester, he was a hero, a brave and conscientious soldier who won the Military Cross and was wounded more than once. As Camus said in his *Carnets* – maybe courage is not enough, but you can only advance that view after you have proved your own courage. I mentioned this to the poet, and he sniffed. I'm sure he deeply disapproved of Camus, a passionate anti-clerical, but on the other hand he approved the thought.

He loathed the callous incompetence of some Great War generals and politicians because he had served alongside the common soldier. (They called him Mad Jack.)

> He's a jolly old stick, said
> Harry to Jack,
> As they slogged up to Arras
> with rifle and pack.
> But he did for them both
> With his plan of attack.

The anger in his war poems makes them very modern: he wrote them to avenge the fat profiteers at home who 'mock the riddled corpses round Bapaume'. But in a curious sense they were out of key with the rest of his output. They were passionately sincere, of course – I remember him telling me, with a simplicity I found utterly disarming, that 'the Somme was my finest hour' – but in fact I think his fame will ultimately rest on the *Sherston Memoirs*, for the reason that while in his war poems he struggled to integrate soldier's slang into a manner of speaking which was naturally anything but slangy, in the prose memoirs he could speak in his own cultivated and naturally high-poetic voice.

But of course the 'enigma' of Sassoon was his many-sidedness. Not simply versatility: many-sidedness which is not the same thing precisely. Fox-hunter and poet, infantry officer and pacifist, satirist and metaphysical Catholic convert, predator and conservationist – he eluded, in his life and in his work, all glib attempts to pin him down.

When I met him he had made his final move, and Siegfried's Journey was done. He had found his haven. The young infantry officer whose satirical war poems sent eyebrows and blood pressures racing up; the fox-hunting man whose love of horseflesh puzzled the aesthetes; the furious iconoclast who even forty-five years later could not speak of the generals of the First World War without a bewildered anger – this strange bundle of diverse strands had ended up at peace in the embrace of the Roman Catholic Church.

The conversion had been sudden, when it came; yet, with the insufferable clarity of hindsight, one could see it implicit in the unconverted poet. This was the notion that I put to him, tentatively, over tea. He agreed with me that from 1909 to 1960, the same longing voice had spoken in almost every poem. He had always been writing *as if* awaiting the moment when faith should come. In 1924 he could write

> *Alone* ... The word is life endured and known.
> It is the stillness where our spirits walk
> And all but inmost faith is overthrown.

A quarter of a century later the same recognisable voice speaks:

> *I think:* If through some chink in me could shine
> But once – O but one ray
> From that all-hallowing and eternal day,
> Asking no more of heaven I would go hence.

Assenting to this thought, he told me that he gladly acknowledged Hilaire Belloc's proselytising influence. He said that it was while reading a letter from Belloc to Katharine Asquith that he suddenly saw the way clear. 'The metaphor is not that men fall in love with it,' Belloc had written. 'The metaphor is that they discover home. "This was what I sought. This was my need".'

All of that is implicit in every line of the longing poems selected with such insight by the Abbess of Stanbrook. The end was in the beginning.

I showed him a poem which I had selected from *The Power and the Glory* (1925) and suggested that it summed him up. He read it aloud, quietly, and smiled in a deprecatory way. This was the verse:

> Let there be God, say I. And what I've done
> Goes onward like the splendour of the sun
> And rises up in rapture and is one
> With the white power of conscience that commands.

I asked him if he would throw light on what was seen as a paradox – that quite soon after the war, the man who had been a symbol of protesting youth was better known as the elegiac singer of an older order. He replied that he was not simply nostalgic for an old order, but for order itself. Alongside the

Satirical Poems and *Counter-Attack* stand the *Memoirs of a Fox-hunting Man*; alongside the *Memoirs of an Infantry Officer* stand *The Old Huntsman* and *The Weald of Youth*.

To illuminate this paradox, or perhaps it was just to tease me a little, he said, when it came to the question of my taking his photograph, that he believed one side of his face showed the poet Siegfried Sassoon, and the other showed George Sherston, the fox-hunting man. I thought I could detect a difference, but to be on the safe side I photographed them both; and by the time I had dried my prints, back in the cottage at Clandon, I could not distinguish Sherston from Sassoon.

And why should one? Completeness is all. The many-sided man was rooted in the variousness of his living. The memoirs of the soldier, horseman and rebel had sold 500,000 copies; the *Collected Poems* had sold 50,000; there were only 500 copies of *The Path to Peace*. But in a sense, as I suggested to him, this chart of a poet's spiritual pilgrimage encompasses and illuminates the whole of Siegfried's journey, out of the old century, across the weald of youth, over the hard going of middle age to the beckoning coverts wherein he found his peace; galloping and being thrown and always re-mounting, a rare good-plucked 'un, robust and sensitive, brave and kind.

As the hours slipped past, so quickly, we became more friendly and at ease, and he spoke without constraint of little things, homely things. Thin and erect in his faded blazer and sandy breeches, he showed me the two rough-coated mares which roamed in the paddock and which he still rode regularly. He spoke of his son's photographic dark-room up in the attics, and the mention of them reminded him that he had just had to spend £7,000 on the old roof. He spoke of his dead wife, and told me how beautifully she had kept the gardens, neglected then.

He was diffident and courtly, shy and quiet, but very kind to a journalist – and he had suffered from journalists. He was an attentive host and made sure that I had had enough tea, and he was patient and still while I made my photographs, which later appeared in *The Sunday Times*.

I don't think I have ever met a man who gave out such a firm, pervasive impression of inner peace, of stillness at the centre, of spiritual equilibrium. He was undoubtedly one of the greatest men I have met. This memoir is a mere fragment, for my personal contact with him was fragmentary, and I cannot pretend otherwise. But I am proud to have shaken his hand and received his blessing.

18

Henry

HENRY WILLIAMSON is my most distinguished friend, the only friend I have who is indisputably a genius. I have known him as a writer since the late 'Twenties, as a man since the war, as a friend since 1958.

He printed the following epigraphs at the front of his novel *Lucifer Before Sunrise*, one of the last in his great sequence, *A Chronicle of Ancient Sunlight*:

> If a poet is sensitive enough to his
> age, and brave enough to face it directly,
> it will kill him through exacerbation
> of the senses alone
> *Author unknown*

> If ways to the better there be, it
> exacts a full look at the worst
> *Thomas Hardy*

Henry has been brave enough to take that 'full look at the worst'; sensitive enough (and too much) to his age. It has not killed him – he is still hale at seventy-four – but it has pressed out of his exacerbated nervous system some of the most poignant and impassioned writing of our day. I have no doubt that a younger generation will turn to him, as they are turning now to Blake; will acclaim *A Chronicle of Ancient Sunlight* as the great historical novel of the twentieth century.

Far better known at the moment, to most readers, are Henry's 'nature' and animal books: *Tarka the Otter, Salar the Salmon, The Epic of Brock the Badger, Chakchek the Peregrine, Life in a Devon Village, Tales of a Devon Village, The Phasian Bird, Tales of Moorland and Estuary, A Clear Water Stream, The Old Stag, The Peregrine's Saga, The Lone Swallows*. There is no argument about his mastery of this genre. He writes about 'nature' better than any writers since his exemplars, Richard Jefferies and W. H. Hudson – and often better than they did. He is associated in the general mind with Devon, and to a slightly lesser extent Norfolk, where he has spent so many years, farming as well as writing. The intuitive purity, the certainty and mastery of his nature writing are universally acknowledged. They have rarely been equalled, and then only in brief incandescent bursts. His consistency and stamina in the genre are unrivalled.

But his nature writing is only a fraction of his prodigious output, and to Henry, the less important fraction. He has put his life and soul into the immense novel sequence. It is his message to humanity about humanity that he wants to be remembered by.

When I got to know Henry Williamson well he was still living in a hut in a field 560 feet above the estuary of the Twin Rivers, Taw and Torridge. He bought the field for £100 when *Tarka the Otter*, his most famous book, though not his best, won the Hawthornden Prize in 1928.

The hill is crowned with a crest of trees which he planted in 1928. Atlantic gales have worn and whittled them, but they still make a solid windbreak to the north, and below them the goldfinch-haunted field slopes gently and is green.

You turn in through a palisade gate and there is Henry's hut. He built it in 1928 with the help of two local boys, Davy Jones and Lionel Jefferies, who lie in Georgeham Churchyard now, at the bottom of the hill. The hut is about eight feet by ten. The outer walls are made of overlapping planks of elm, cut with the natural curves and bumps of the trunk untrimmed, and pinned to an oak frame. There is a stone fireplace in the corner, and a weathervane in the shape of a salmon. Aptly, for this is the hut in which *Salar the Salmon* was written. A book which the Sitwells ridiculed, but which I think a greater book than *Tarka*; a book of marvellous poetic insight and stern discipline.

When I entered the numinous hut, Henry's scythe blade and bow saw hung on the walls, with line-driers, and a photograph of infantrymen at Cambrai. Carpenter's tools were neatly stacked in slots at the back of the workbench. There was a cupboard, a leather-seated chair and a neat, narrow, spartan bed. All these things told the visitor something incontrovertible about the man who lived in the hut at Ox's Cross.

In fact there were (and are) two more huts now, newer erections, spaced out in an arc along the curving line of his trees. The hermit's home had become a settlement, a kraal. To get from one 'room' to another you swished through scythed, ankle-deep grass. But it all began with that one little hut, the hut which *Tarka* bought, the hut in which *Salar* was born.

At this time I had known Henry, off and on and in a mainly professional sense, for many years; but I had not yet got to know him as a friend. A little book had just been published called *A Clear Water Stream*. When I read an advance copy I realised not only that it was in the direct tradition of *Tarka* and *Salar* and *Tales of Moorland and Estuary* and the other great early books of 'nature', but also that it revealed a good bit more about the great writer who had turned from 'nature writing' to something far more controversial; and, brooding over the fluctuating fortunes and critical reputation of a man whom I had not seen for years, but had always venerated, I asked him to receive me in his home.

'Do come,' he replied. 'We will enjoy ourselves.'

He was then sixty-two. I had not seen him since he was about fifty. But he was apparently unchanged. I have always found him apparently unchanged. His hair had turned white but he was still erect, slim, quick and apparently tireless. I never knew anyone with more nervous energy and stamina – except Harold Evans. Henry still had, he always had, he will always have that visionary eye.

He was awaiting me in the lane by his palisade gate and he was using the waiting time to trim his hedge, with a bill hook. He was an expert countryman, not an amateur. He was smoking his small pipe. There was that moment I know so well, the moment that has come and gone so often, a moment of suspense when the mutual shyness battles with the mutual curiosity; but it passed almost immediately, and with its passing we passed from casual acquaintance to something else. As the years have proven.

Remember that I came to Ox's Cross as a visitor from that 'London' world that had for years neglected, misused and (I think) misunderstood Henry Williamson. For a dozen years at least he had lived like a hermit in his field, unsought by the smart literary world, slogging away with a sort of desperate proud humility at his prodigious output. He is the most meticulous perfectionist I ever knew. He wrote *Tarka* seventeen times, mostly at night after a day's work on the farm, sitting in the kitchen by candlelight, with a sick child in his arms. He can hardly have forgotten that after 1928 the greatest were quick to call him *genius*. Arnold Bennett could not praise him too highly – as a novelist. Thomas Hardy and John Galsworthy did him honour. Then the Second World War nearly broke him: his friendship with Sir Oswald Mosley, his detention under Regulation 18B, his so-called ambivalence towards fascism and the Germans, which sprang from his torments of insight, suffering and sympathy in the First World War, turned many against him. It was indeed the long dark night of the soul; but, as he told me, he came to realise that this cathartic experience helped him to harmonise the diverse impulses of his chameleon-like nature.

We drove over to the headland, all packed into my pretty little car, and to amuse his young son Harry, Henry made little jokes of a sort which instantly endeared him to me all afresh, jokes that were in my own sense *silly*, you had to be a happy simpleton to appreciate them. Such as 'Mirling Stoss at the wheel' when I took a hairpin bend with a great display of sharp gear-changing and elbow flashing. Mirling Stoss. Stirling Moss. Henry looked a little abashed, as if he feared I might make a note of it and use it against him. Since it was exactly the sort of thing I'd say myself, I felt more and more at ease. Little Harry was delighted: Mirling Stoss I remained.

We walked over to Baggy, the jutting headland, to picnic on the close-cropped grass above a wrinkling, cloud-shadowed sea, and we could look across the bay to the deep, twisting gully, now choked with blackthorn, down which Tarka slid to the sea.

All this time in the light summer air of afternoon we were relaxing towards each other. Henry who had known me only as his features editor on various papers was beginning to feel free with me as a human being, not a probing monster out to outrage his inner integrity. I was getting over my natural awe of the writer whom I so much admired and was coming to be at ease with him as a relaxed companion, one I could make little jokes with, drink with, be at ease. After tea we had a drink of beer at a pub where he knew a raven.

Later we ate a meal beginning with Mrs Williamson's delicious cabbage-and-potato soup, followed by steak and wine. Henry had laid in claret against my coming, but it turned out sharp and acidulous. I could see that he was upset, and it might have developed into sadness; little things sometimes do; but we discovered a bottle of sweet port wine and we drank that instead, growing happy. As night fell, cool and calm, blackbirds chakkered derisively at an owl that was poaching in the dense trees, the lamps of Appledore glittered below, and Hartland Light flashed through the pines.

To honour a guest and delight a boy, Henry had built a great bonfire in the field, and now he lit it – with one match, without paper: he is a wonderfully neat, tidy and competent man; all his vast store of manuscripts in flawless order, even when living in a field. We stood warming ourselves at the blaze while sparks shot crackling skywards like tracer. In the leaping light he looked like a boy again, wholly immersed in the sensual young moment, the eternal moment. Then he quoted, standing there in the field as the flames leaped, from his favourite Francis Thompson, the stanza which begins:

> Beware the black rider, through blasted dreams
> borne nightly,
> Saved you bin, from Venus Queen, and the dead
> that die unrightly ...

and again his face fell into the stern and stoic lines of the mystic which at heart he is.

When the fire had gone down and young Harry had gone to bed, Henry read to us a chapter from the next-to-be-published novel in his great sequence, *A Chronicle of Ancient Sunlight*:

the novel called *Love and the Loveless*. His mobile features were animated as he acted out the dialogue. Then it was time for bed. He lit a fire of twigs for me in the magic hut where *Salar* was written, in pain, and before it had died down I was sleeping where Lawrence of Arabia had slept before me.

Henry woke me with a mug of tea. A gallon can of water stood by the open door. I poured some into a bowl in a tripod standing in the wet grass of the field, and washed in the open air.

Then it was porridge and coffee and farewell, and the long ride home across the great plain of England, brilliant in the foliage of May, thinking about greatness and reputation, which are not necessarily the same thing.

'Everybody' knows Henry Williamson as the greatest English writer on the natural creation since Jefferies and Hudson. But the passion to tie neat exclusive labels on an artist misfires disastrously with him. Though the best of the nature writing is imperishable, there is a good sporting chance that it is as a Tolstoyan novelist that posterity will appraise him, surprised as posterity is so often surprised by the blindness and wilful neglect of his contemporaries. The tormented, loving and indefatigable soldier-novelist is a visionary whose vision does not stop short at the natural creation. I think I know why some of the novels failed to win the recognition he might have hoped for – to put it in a word, there is a bit too much technical farming in them, which might with advantage have been taken out for the general reader as well as for the literary critic – but time will make that less of a drawback, not more. He creates his own atmosphere of pervasive drama and sensuous experience if he is describing an event as superficially undramatic as the kindling of a fire. Every minute you live with him. Every page tells you more about the tortured perfectionist – and about the England he has loved. I believe that one day the hut in the field called Ox's Cross will be a place of pilgrimage.

*   *   *

Over the years since that sojourn at Ox's Cross I have seen Henry in various locations, but the milieu never matters. He came to see us at our old cottage in Clandon. He turned up at our slightly less ancient cottage that nestled at the end of a lonely rutted track in Sussex, the cottage from which no other habitation was visible, the cottage that had its back to the dark woods named Hope Rough and Songhurst Furze. We have eaten out in restaurants and pubs, we have shared meals at his London club. And constantly there has been that flow of wonderful revealing letters, letters I would not dream of quoting, letters from the heart.

I think I know Henry fairly well, now. He bought a house in Ilfracombe, where he is often visited by young readers who have perceived – what some of their elders failed to perceive – the essential flame that burns in his unconquerable heart. From that house he sends little to the printer, these days: the vast novel sequence is ended, it ended in tears: but he sends out occasional messages, written in his tiny beautiful hand, a handwriting so sensitive yet so firm you can imagine the hand and the heart that direct the pen. Letters of unimaginable candour, letters that sear the heart. Yes, I think I know him fairly well.

He isn't an easy man to know. His memory rides him, he remembers everything, for ever – every insult, every misunderstanding, every detail of every enterprise that turned sour – as well as all those magical moments when, seared to the soul by the years in Flanders, he settled in a cottage in Devon to celebrate the glories of the natural creation. In *A Chronicle of Ancient Sunlight* he has celebrated his generation, the lost generation; he has placed it in its historical context, most poignantly; he has made his great echoing call for love.

His daemon drives him. He could not be otherwise. It can't be easy to be so sensitive, so remembering, so demanding, so loving and generous and at the same time so insistent on his own way of perfectionism. He is a grand man, and difficult – yet in another sense, he is wonderfully easy, full of jokes and the nice trivial fun of ordinary people. I don't suppose any two people who know him would describe him in identical terms. He is a chameleon-like character, as I said. A bundle of qualities which seem contradictory. But all this will be unimportant, as the future unrolls. When everyone who knew him, or claimed to know him, or knew an aspect or two of him, are dead, his books will remain. Visionary books, books of a poet with a flame in his heart, a poet who never wrote a verse. Time will sift. The flame will burn more brightly.

I will indulge myself with one quotation from a letter which Henry Williamson wrote to me, not long ago. 'Thank you,' he wrote, 'for your staunch friendship.'

I could not end on a prouder note.